INTRODUCTION TO INFORMATION AND COMPUTER LITERACY

with Microsoft Windows 95
and Microsoft Office 97

RON GILSTER

CONNIE GLEASON

JOE BUSH

INTRODUCTION TO INFORMATION AND COMPUTER LITERACY

with Microsoft Windows 95
and Microsoft Office 97

RON GILSTER

CONNIE GLEASON

JOE BUSH

toExcel

San Jose   New York   Lincoln   Shanghai

INTRODUCTION TO
INFORMATION AND COMPUTER
LITERACY

For information address:

toExcel

165 West 95th Street, Suite B-N

New York, NY 10025

www.toExcel.com

Published by toExcel, a division of Kaleidoscope Software, Inc.

Marca registrada
toExcel
New York, NY

ISBN: 1-58348-101-x

Library of Congress Card Catalogue Number: 98-88495

Printed in the United States of America

0 9 8 7 6 5 4 3 2 1

NOTE TO INSTRUCTORS

We thank and congratulate you on your vision and commitment to contextual learning and the value of computer and information literacy to the future success of your students.

This book was created as a way for students to learn computer and information literacy using an applied contextual method. We believe that this approach is more meaningful to the student than that used in other introductory computer skill-based texts.

With the exception of the Windows lessons, previous versions of Word and Excel may work for the lessons in this book. However, the lessons have been tested using only the versions shown.

Ron, Connie, & Joe

TABLE OF CONTENTS

INTRODUCTION

Over the past twenty years, there has been an explosion of technology in the information processing and communications areas. The technological advances have deeply impacted our society changing forever the way we access information and communicate. Books, still a valuable and important source of information, are no longer the only information source on any given topic. In the past, the telephone was used to talk to some-body at a distance, but it is no longer the only way you can "talk" with someone. Technology has providing tools such as the Internet, the fax machine, CD-ROM and DVD, interactive video teleconferencing, and so on.

It is estimated that everything we know - all of our accumulat-ed knowledge from the past 5,000 years or so - can be stored on a few hundred compact disks. Because of technology, our knowledge is now increasing faster and faster. The challenge this represents to students and researchers remains the same - finding and interpreting the information. Fortunately, tech-nology has also provided a set of tools to retrieve and categorize information and present it to others. The personal computer and its software tools, such as word processing, electronic spreadsheet, electronic mail, and Internet access software are now the primary tools for personal information processing.

The ability to process data into information on the computer has become one of the most important communications skills you can learn. Computer and information literacy are basic communication skills and, in most cases, an occupational skill as well.

The computer is everywhere. It is used in just about every job or occupation. Learning to use the computer to process and access information is especially important to students. The computer helps you do research in your school or local library as well as libraries around your county, state, country and the world. It can also allow you to discuss issues with your classmates or perhaps experts in your field of study. The computer can then aid you to produce and publish a high-quality document. It has software tools such as a spelling checker, a grammar checker, a thesaurus, and charting, drawing and graphic tools that help you to organize and prepare your document. Of course, you must still provide the words and ideas for your documents.

Being computer and information literate - knowing how to use the computer and its programs to produce quality results - allows you to focus on your message. When you write a letter or a report by hand, you must use caution and concentrate on the appearance of your document as you write. When using a typewriter, you must be mindful of the keys you are pressing and the spelling and spacing of the words and paragraphs being created. However, the computer and its software tools, when applied correctly and appropriately, allow you to concentrate on the words, ideas, and concepts of your document. After you've completed your message, you can check the document for spelling, editing, proofreading or you can add special features.

Welcome to the world of information. The lessons you perform in this book are designed to provide you with two sets of essential skills: the ability to prepare a finished document on the computer, and the ability to choose and apply the appropriate computer tools. It is this combination of essential communications skills that is your ticket to the world of information and the future.

What You Will Learn

This book emphasizes several of the information processing and document preparation skills you will need to produce quality documents. The overall goals of this book are to:

- ❖ Explain the various components of the computer system and how each is used

❖   Show how the computer and its software tools are applied to produce a product - a research paper

❖   Introduce you to the Internet, its vast amounts of information resources and the tools used to access these resources

Each of the software packages covered in this book has many more features than are presented. We have included only the software functions and features you need to accomplish the goals stated above. While the more advanced features of the software packages can provide you with greater usability and flexibility, they are not needed at this time. To get a basic understanding of how to use the computer, you don't need to learn all of these features in the beginning. Later, after you have mastered the fundamental skills included in this book, you may wish to look for more advanced courses to gain a complete understanding of each piece of software.

The application software tools used in this book are the Microsoft Windows 95 operating environment and the Microsoft Office 97 applications: Word 8.0 and Excel 8.0.

Organization

This book is organized into a series of 30 to 60 minute lessons. Each lesson emphasizes a specific set of skills or knowledge. The lessons are arranged so you will learn the specific hardware and software as needed to complete a project. The book uses the metaphor of producing a research paper as the context of when hardware and software features are needed. In short, you learn what to do when it is time to do it. We hope that presenting the lessons in this way will help you get a better understanding of why and when you would use a feature.

We recommend that you read each lesson completely before starting it. This will help you to understand the purpose of the lesson and the terms or processes you will be learning. Then follow the lesson's instructions as you work on the computer. Compare your results (outputs) to the examples shown in the lesson. If your work matches our example, then you've performed the steps correctly. If not, you should study the lesson steps to find where you may have gone wrong. In the worst case, you may need to begin the lesson again.

Some lessons refer to a student disk. Your instructor or lab monitor can help you to locate the files you need.

At the end of each lesson is a **Things to Remember** exercise. The questions, word lists, and exercises are included to review the important concepts, terms, features, or functions of each lesson. Take the time to do this review. It will help you in later lessons. Each review also provides a reminder of the important points from each lesson.

When you've completed all of the lessons, you will have accomplished each of the steps needed to produce a research. You will have created text, formatted the text, edited the text, checked the spelling, inserted a table and a graphic, added headers, footers and page numbers to the document, added **bold** and <u>underlined</u> font features, used the Internet to do research, and prepared a works cited (bibliography) page. All of these tasks will have been done using the computer and software. We believe this set of skills should be useful to you throughout your school and work careers, as well as in everyday use as well.

Credits

The software used in the lessons is the same software used to produce this book. Word 97 was used for all of the word processing and Excel 97 was used to create all of the spreadsheets and charts. Some additional software was used in special cases: Paint Shop Pro, Version 5, from JASC, Inc. was used to capture, create, or enhance the graphics images. Apple Computer, Inc., IBM Corporation, Intel Corporation, and the

Hewlett Packard Corporation supplied the public domain images of the computer hardware. Our thanks to these fine companies for their outstanding products and assistance.

Our Thanks

We hope you find the lessons in this book helpful in becoming computer and information literate.

Good Luck!

Ron Gilster, Connie Gleason, & Joe Bush

SECTION 1

COMPUTER HARDWARE

The **personal computer (PC)** is a combination of electronic components that work together to form a system. It is the general purpose of this system to make the computer useful to you - the user. The electronic parts of the computer can be categorized into two general groups: the hardware and the software.

The **hardware** is the physical equipment of the computer. The **software** is the electronically stored instructions for the computer. You will learn more about the computer's software in later lessons. In this section you will learn about the computer's hardware.

This section contains three lessons:

❖ The first lesson acquaints you with the names of the various parts of the computer itself

❖ The second lesson explains the keyboard and the various keys on the keyboard and their uses

❖ The third lesson introduces you to floppy disks and preparing a floppy disk to use with a computer

Included in each lesson are a number of valuable terms and definitions These terms are valuable because they appear throughout the remaining lessons. At the end of each lesson is a **Things to Remember** exercise. Each of these exercises contains a list of the terms, items or actions you should review for understanding.

LESSON 1
IDENTIFYING THE HARDWARE

There are many different kinds of computers with each type of computer designed for a particular task. Some computers are built into other products, such as a microwave oven, or an automobile, or even a television set. Large computer systems are used in businesses, hospitals, and governments to process large databases and make complex computations. However, the computer you are probably most familiar with is the personal computer or as it is commonly called, the **PC**.

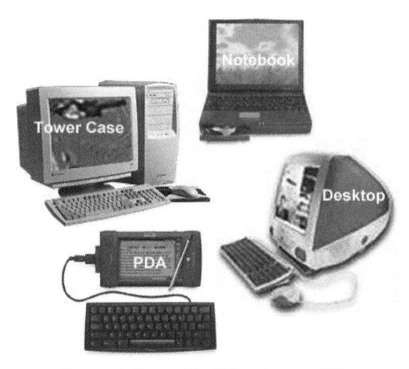

Figure 1-1: Some of the Different types of PCs

Personal computers are also available in many different types. A few of the different types of PCs are shown in Figure 1-1. Some users prefer the added power of a large tower unit and others like the convenience of a laptop or notebook unit. However, the most common form of a PC is the desktop computer. The desktop computer is the type of computer found in schools, businesses and in homes. The desktop computer consists of a system unit which sits on the desktop horizontally. The PC monitor sits on the system unit. The keyboard and mouse are usually located in front of the system unit. Figure 1-2 illustrates the setup of a desktop PC.

Figure 1-2: A Desktop PC

In the lessons on this book, we will be referring to the desktop unit unless otherwise indicated.

Note to student:

The activities in this section are marked with either a pointing finger symbol or a mouse unit symbol.

☞ The pointing finger indicates an action or exercise that involves the computer, one of its components, or an outside activity, like the one that follows below.

✆ The mouse unit symbol indicates an exercise that requires you to enter data or interact with the computer in another way.

✆ Sit in front of a computer (the one you will use to perform the lessons in this book would be the best choice), while you read the following system component descriptions. As you read each description, locate the hardware component on your computer system. Use the illustration in Figure 1-3 for reference.

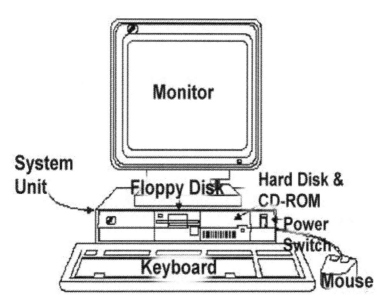

Figure 1-3: Common Personal Computer Components

System Unit

The computer's main component is called the **system unit** (Figure 1-4). It contains the computer's **electronic** circuits, connections, and storage devices and is the part of the computer that is located inside the case. Inside the system unit is the hard disk, floppy disk, CD-ROM, speaker, memory, lights, and all of the other electronic parts of the computer.

Figure 1-4: A System Unit

Disk drives

Disk drives are permanent data storage devices that store your data on special disks. There are three basic types of disk drives:

- ❖ The hard disk
- ❖ The floppy disk
- ❖ The CD-ROM

The **hard disk**, shown in Figure 1-5, gets its name from the fact that the disks used to store data are rigid. It can store up to billions of characters and is a very fast and reliable internal storage device. A disadvantage to using the hard disk for storage is that it is not portable and usually stays inside the system unit.

Figure 1-5: A Hard Disk Drive with Its Cover Removed

Figure 1-6: A Floppy Disk Drive Unit

The **floppy disk**, which is also called a diskette, is the removable and portable permanent data storage for the computer. A floppy disk can store as much as 1.4 million characters of data using either the 5 ¼ inch or 3 ½ inch floppy disk. Figure 1-6 shows a floppy disk drive removed from the system unit. Normally, only the front of the floppy disk drive is exposed on the front of the computer.

Figure 1-7: An External CD-ROM Drive

The CD-ROM (Compact Disk - Read Only Memory), as shown in Figure 1-7, that is used on the computer is very similar to the CDs used for music and video. In fact, most computers will play music or video CDs. A CD becomes a CD-ROM when computer data is stored on it. A CD-ROM will store up to 650 million characters of data. It is a portable storage media that can only be read. However, there are newer CD-ROM drives that can also write to a CD.

Disk Drive Designators

The computer's disk drives (floppy disk, hard disk, and CD-ROM) are designated by a letter code followed by a colon, for example - **A:** (notice that there is no space between the letter and the colon). The computer recognizes this combination as the name of a disk drive. The most common disk drive designations are:

A: The first and primary floppy disk drive on the computer

B: The second floppy disk drive on the computer

C: The first and primary hard disk drive on the computer

D: The CD-ROM or a second hard disk

E:, F:, G:, etc. Used for a variety of storage or connectors such as a Zip drive, tape drive, or a network connection.

Power Switch

The **power switch** does just what you would expect - it turns the computer's power on and off. When you flip the power switch to the "on" position, the computer performs a "cold start" or "cold boot." This means the computer is starting itself from a "cold" or powered off status. The term "boot" comes from the word bootstrap, as in "pulling oneself up by one's own boot-straps" or self-starting.

Occasionally, you may need to use the power switch to restart your computer when the system fails or locks up. The computer can fail for a variety of reasons, none of which are important at this time. When we discuss the basic concepts of Windows 95 later in the book, you will learn other ways that you can use to restart the computer should it fail to function properly.

Other Devices

Although not integrated into it, most people often think of the monitor, keyboard and mouse as components of the system unit.

Monitor

The **monitor** is also called the display or the screen. It is the primary output device for the computer. The computer displays the results of its actions temporarily on the video display for the user to see. The monitor uses a cathode ray tube to create a television-style display as illustrated by the following picture.

Figure 1-8: A Common PC Monitor

The computer displays its actions, options, and results on its monitor. Nearly all monitors look about the same on the outside, see Figure 1-8, except for their size. It is on the inside, that they differ. Just like television sets are available in different size and picture quality, so are monitors.

Keyboard

The **keyboard** is the primary input device for the computer. Pictures of the two most popular styles are shown in Figure 1-9, the standard or 101-key type on the left and the natural type, also called ergonomic, on the right. Until the computer can understand our spoken commands (probably not all that far off), we will use some form of a keyboard to enter commands and data. Lesson 2 provides more details about the keyboard.

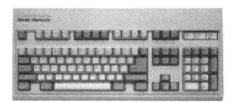 

Figure 1-9 Left: A standard PC 101 Keyboard
Figure 1-9 Right: A Natural or Ergonomic Keyboard Style

Other Input Devices

There are other types of input devices being used with computers as well. For example, **pen-based** computers, called personal digital assistants (PDA) like the one shown in Figure 1-10, use a pen or stylus as its input device. The user uses the pen to enter handwriting, which the computer translates into text.

Pen-based input devices have not been adapted to the desktop personal computer yet. But, eventually this, or a similar technology, may ease the task of entering data into the computer. For now, the keyboard continues to be the most common way of entering data into the computer.

Figure 1-10: A Pen-Based Personal Digital Assistant

Mouse

Another primary device on the computer is the **mouse**, which is used to select and highlight objects on the computer monitor. The common computer mouse has two buttons and is connected to the system unit by a wire "tail." In Lesson 5, you will take a more detailed look at the mouse and other pointing devices.

Figure 1-11: The Common Two-Button Mouse (Microsoftus Billii Gatesius)

Inside the System Unit

Located inside the system unit are electronic circuits that perform the instructions and process the data you give the computer. These circuits are extremely small, even microscopic, and have names like microprocessor, integrated circuit, and circuit board. Exactly what each of these mysterious devices is and does is not essential to learning to your computer literacy, much like you don't need to understand the internal combustion engine to drive a car. However, you should have some understanding of the components inside the system unit to have some understanding of how the computer works.

Figure 1-12: The Pentium Pro Microprocessor

Microprocessor

The primary electronic component in the computer is an integrated circuit called the **microprocessor**, like the one shown in Figure 1-12. An integrated circuit is a very complex electronic component that contains millions of tiny electronic circuits. The microprocessor is why the personal computer is also called a microcomputer. It uses a microprocessor to carry out your instructions. The microprocessor and its supporting electronic circuitry is also called the central processing unit or CPU.

Figure 1-13: A PC Motherboard

The CPU and the remainder of the electronic components of the computer are all located inside the system unit on an electronic circuit board known affectionately as the **motherboard**, see Figure 1-13. The motherboard contains virtually all of the electronic components that perform the task of computing. Located on the motherboard are the microprocessor, memory, ROM, and all of the other circuits that keep processing coordinated.

If the motherboard also contains the video and audio circuits, it becomes known as a system board. This is because all of the main processing units are present on the single board.

Memory

As mentioned above, the motherboard also hosts another very important part of the computer - the computer's **memory**. Computers use two separate types of storage: temporary storage (memory), and permanent storage (floppy disks, hard disk, and CD-ROM). Of the two storage types, temporary storage is the most important to the computer's operation. Without memory, the computer is not able to store the data you enter or carry out your commands. Memory provides temporarily storage for the computer's instructions and data for the CPU.

There are two types of memory: ROM and RAM. Both are equally important to the operation of the computer, but at different times and in different ways.

ROM

ROM is short for read-only-memory. ROM is the type of memory that cannot be changed. It can be read, but not written to. This protects its contents from being destroyed or altered. ROM storage is **static** in that it does not lose its contents when the power is turned off. This type of memory is also called **nonvolatile**. ROM contains the instructions the computer needs to do its boot sequence. As explained before, the boot process starts the computer when the power is turned on.

RAM

The second type of memory is **RAM** or random-access-memory. This is a fancy way of saying that it can be changed. RAM can be both written and read. RAM is the computer's temporary storage - the "memory" mentioned above. The computer temporarily stores all data and instructions in RAM before and after each is used. RAM contains all of the data and programs that are active and in use by the computer at any one time.

However, RAM is **dynamic**. This means that it loses its contents when its power is interrupted for any reason. If the computer's power is turned off, or even briefly interrupted, all of RAM is erased. When this happens, all of the data and programs stored in RAM are gone and must be reentered or restarted.

RAM works a lot like the children's toy called a "magic slate." You can write on it all you want, but if you lift the cellophane cover page, the wax impression image is erased. You can start programs, enter data, and store whatever you want in RAM, but if the power goes off, its images (data and instructions) are erased. Another term for this is **volatile**.

How your data and instructions get into RAM is really quite simple. When you turn on the computer, the instructions stored in the ROM carry out the boot sequence. One of the steps in the boot sequence is to start the operating system running. For example, when you start Windows 95, its instructions are copied from the hard disk into RAM. The CPU then begins to execute these instructions one at a time. Any data you may enter using the keyboard or movements of the mouse are first stored in RAM and then displayed on the monitor.

The amount of RAM in a PC directly effects its performance. As a general rule, you can never have too much memory, but most current computers will not address more than four billion bits of memory. Memory is added to the computer by inserting memory modules, like the one in Figure 1-14, into special slots on the motherboard.

Figure 1-14: A PC Memory Module

Peripherals

Beyond the monitor, keyboard, and mouse, there are other devices, called **peripherals**, that provide a means for specialized functions and output processing. These are things such as printers, sound systems, and modems. Peripheral devices (which technically include the monitor, keyboard, and mouse) allow the user to customize the system to fit his or her personal needs.

One person may think a 30-watt sound system is an essential part of a computer. Another may want no sound, but need a very fast color laser printer. Still another may want all of that plus full-motion video conferencing and high-speed data communications. That's the beauty of peripheral devices: they allow you to custom fit your computer to your own particular computing needs.

By adding a special type of electronic circuit, called an expansion card, to the motherboard, you can add peripheral devices to your computer system. Expansion cards plug into expansion slots on the motherboard as shown in Figure 1-15. The peripheral device is then attached to the computer by cables that plug into the expansion cards through special slots on the back of the system unit.

Figure 1-15: The Expansion Slots on a Motherboard

☞ Look at the back of your computer. Each peripheral device is attached to the computer through a cable which plugs into a connector mounted on the expansion card installed inside the system unit. You should find a cables for the monitor, the mouse, and a network connection at minimum. Have you instructor explain which peripherals are being attached to your computer by the cables you find.

Speakers

At a minimum, your computer has a single low-grade **speaker** located inside the system unit that is used to produce beeps and other sounds. Some PCs, like the one in Figure 1-16, have more elaborate speaker systems - some complete with full-sized woofers and sub-woofers - and can play a full range of sound. This requires a sound card be installed in an expansion slot.

Figure 1-16: An Example of a PC with Speakers

Caution

As a beginning computer user, you should not open the computer's system unit. Mechanical or electronic component problems or failures should be diagnosed and repaired only by a trained computer service technician.

Things to Remember

Terms

Define or explain the function of each of the following terms, actions, or descriptors:

A:	Floppy disk
B:	Hard disk
C:	Keyboard
CD-ROM	Microprocessor
Dynamic	Memory
E:, F: G:, etc.	Monitor
Electronic	Mouse

Motherboard

Non-volatile

PC

Pen-based input

Peripherals

Power Switch

RAM

ROM

Speakers

Static

System unit

Volatile

LESSON 2
THE KEYBOARD

The computer **keyboard** is the primary input device for the PC. There are many types of input devices that can be used to enter data into the computer, depending on the type of data to be collected. For example, a thermometer collects data regarding the temperature of the air around it; an altimeter collects data about the altitude of an object; and a clock inputs the current time. These mechanisms are used as input devices because they are able to collect and convert a specific type of data for the computer's use.

The computer keyboard collects data from its users' brains and until the time when the computer can hear and convert our spoken words (not too far away), the keyboard will likely remain the most common and frequently used input device. Input devices are being developed to allow users to enter their handwriting instead of using a keyboard. But for large volume data entry, the keyboard, like that in Figure 2-1, is our mainstay.

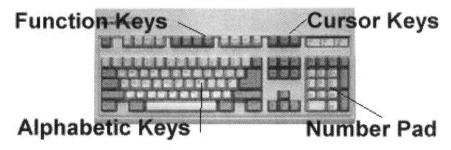

Figure 2-1: Standard Keyboard Groupings

Figure 2-1 shows an example of a standard keyboard. As indicated, the standard computer keyboard is divided into four groups of keys:

❖   the alphabetic and special character keys;

❖   the function keys;

❖   the cursor control keys; and

❖   the number keypad.

In this lesson you will be introduced to the keyboard so that you can identify, locate, and understand each key's action and use.

The Alphabetic Keys

The **alphabetic and special character keys** on the standard keyboard resemble the keys of a typewriter. Included in this group of keys are the upper and lower case letters of the alphabet, the numbers one to zero, the space bar, and a group of special characters.

As listed in Table 2-1, and read left to right at the top of the alphabetic keys on most keyboards, the special characters are: ` ~ @ # $ % ^ & * ( ) - _ = and +.

Also included are the keys that control character spacing (Tab, Enter, and Backspace keys), character case (Shift and Caps Lock keys), and special commands to the computer (Control and Alt keys).

Char.	Name	Key Combination Used
`	Apostrophe	Unshifted key to left of the "1"
~	tilde	Shift + apostrophe key
!	exclamation mark	Shift + 1 key
@	at sign	Shift + 2 key
#	pound sign or number sign	Shift + 3 key
$	dollar sign	Shift + 4 key
%	percent sign	Shift + 5 key
^	carat	Shift + 6 key
&	ampersand	Shift + 7 key
*	asterisk	Shift + 8 key
(	left or open parenthesis	Shift + 9 key
)	right or close parenthesis	Shift + 0 key
-	Hyphen or dash or minus sign	Key to right of 0 key
	Underscore	Shift + hyphen key
=	equal sign	Key to right of hyphen key
+	plus sign	Shift + equal sign key

Table 2-1. Special Character Keys on the Standard Computer Keyboard

The Cursor

Before we go too much further, you should understand the role of the cursor. The **cursor** marks the location of the **insertion point**. The insertion point marks the place where the next character typed will appear. It is normally in the form of a flashing vertical bar as shown in Figure 2-2.

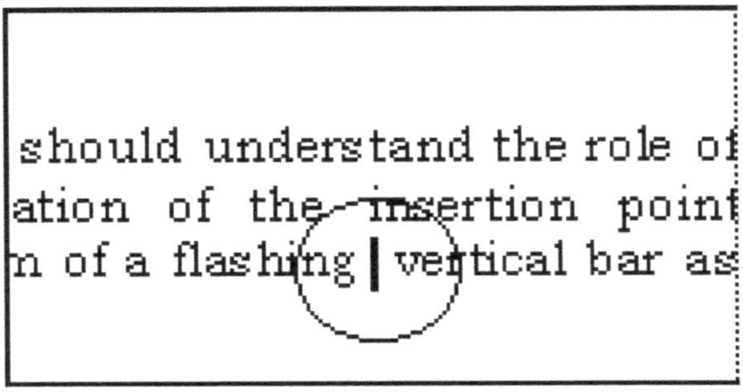

Figure 2-2: The Cursor and Insertion Point (in circle)

The cursor marks where the next character or action entered will take place. The cursor can be moved to the point at which you wish to take an action, insert a character, delete a character, etc. In short, the cursor marks your place as you work in a document.

☞ At the computer you will be using throughout the book, locate the following keys:

Tab

The Tab key moves the cursor insertion point a preset number of spaces, usually one-half inch. When the Tab key is used with the Shift key, the insertion point moves backward, which is to the left, the same number of preset positions.

Shift

This key is used to shift the alphabetic keys into uppercase and the number keys to their respective special characters. Holding down the Shift key while pressing a character key causes the key's shifted character to be entered. If you use the Shift key with the letter "a," an upper-case A will be entered and displayed. Without depressing the Shift key, the resulting letter is unchanged and you get a lowercase a.

The Shift key is also used to access the top symbol on those keys which have two characters. For example, without the Shift key, any of the number keys enter the number value for the key pressed. With the Shift key pressed, the upper or special character on that key is entered. Without the Shift key, pressing the 4 key results in the number 4 (Mr. Obvious strikes again). With the Shift key down, depressing the 4 key enters a dollar sign ($).

Caps Lock

This key works like the Shift-Lock key on a typewriter. When pressed, it locks the shift key function into place. The Caps Lock key only affects the alphabetic characters on the keyboard. The number and special characters are unaffected by the Caps Lock key.

When the Caps Lock key is engaged, the action of the Shift key is reversed. If you press the "a" key with the Caps Lock engaged, it results in an uppercase A, exactly what you expected. However, while the Caps Lock key is engaged, if you hold down the Shift key and then press the "a" key, you will get a lower case a - the Shift key reverses the effect of the Caps Lock key.

On most keyboards an indicator light on the keyboard is lighted when the Caps Lock key is engaged. This indicator is usually in the upper right corner, above the numeric key pad, on most keyboards.

The Caps Lock keys action is called a **toggle**. Pressing it locks its function "on" and pressing it again unlocks the function and turns it "off." The first time you press the Caps Lock key, it locks the alphabetic keyboard into uppercase letters and lights the indicator light. The second time you press it, it is toggled so the shift is reversed and the indicator light goes off. There are several toggle keys and switches on the keyboard. We will discuss some others later in this lesson.

The Control Key

The Control key (sometimes marked "Ctrl") is used with other keys to enter short-cut commands and directions. For example, pressing the Control key and the letter "C" key at the same time tells Windows 95 and most Windows-compatible software to "copy" a selected object to the Windows Clipboard. Each software application may have a different meaning for the control key and its combinations, but most Windows 95 programs are use generally the same meanings. As you work with more application software, you will become aware of come control key uses.

The Alt Key

The "Alt" key is also used together with other keys to enter "alternate" key values or commands to software. It works very similar to the control key. One very common use for the Alt key is to gain access to application menus without the mouse.

The Backspace Key

This key, located in the upper-right corner of the alphabetic keyboard, is marked with the word "Backspace." Occasionally, it is marked with only an arrow pointing to the left (←) . When pressed, it covers the character to the left of the cursor with the character to the right of the cursor. In effect, it deletes the location to the left of the cursor and its contents.

You should not use the backspace key to move the cursor because it always removes the characters in its path.

The Enter key

This key is probably the most used key on the PC keyboard. It is used for a number of related actions, depending upon the software in use. When you press the Enter key, you are telling the computer one of three things:

1. You've completed your entry.

     or

2. You wish to end a line of type or a paragraph.

     or

3. You wish to enter a blank line.

The Enter key has these three functions regardless of the application you are using. As you use the Enter key, reflect on which of these actions you are taking.

Function Keys

☞ Continue locating keys on the keyboard:

The next group of keys allows you to communicate special pre-set commands to the computer and its software As you will see in later lessons, Windows 95, Word and Excel each assign different functions to these keys.

Figure 2-3: Function Keys

As shown in Figure 2-3, **function keys** are marked F1 through F12. The "function" assigned to each key is set by the active software. While some function key assignments have become standardized, you should not assume that every program uses them the same. It would certainly be easier if all software assigned the exact same meanings and activities to the function keys, but since no two pieces of software perform the same task in exactly the same manner, it is not practical. As you become more familiar with the computer, you will appreciate that using the same functions in every program is not as easy as it sounds.

Function keys are also used as short cut or hot-keys. This allows you to request an action or feature without having to type a command or click an icon. Function keys can also be used together with other keys to allow you to select more than one action from an individual function key. For example, when working in a word processing program, it would be difficult for the software to know whether the word "save" was meant as a command or as part of a sentence describing a cause. So, in addition to menu choices, hot-keys are set up by the software that allow commands to be chosen; in this case the F12 key begins the "Save As" action.

Escape Key

Located at the extreme left of the function keys is the key commonly labeled as **"Esc,"** the **Escape key**. In many, but not all, instances it is used to cancel the last command or action you've chosen or selected. You will have cause to use it in later lessons.

Cursor Keys

Cursor keys, also called **cursor control keys**, allow you to reposition the cursor and the insertion point within a document. This allows you more control for editing, formatting, and special actions on the text or images of the file. As shown in Figure 2-4, these keys are located in the middle section of the keyboard as shown in Figure 2-4. This group also includes keys to control the typing mode, capture the screen image, control the movement of the display, and interrupt the action of the computer.

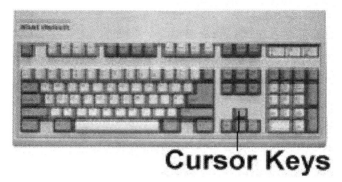

Cursor Keys

Figure 2-4: Cursor Control Keys

Some keyboards may have two of some of the keys. For now, focus on those in the Cursor keys section of the keyboard. The duplicates will be explained later.

Insert or Ins Key

Like the Caps Lock key, the **Insert key** is a toggle key. When pressed, it switches the entry mode between type-over (replace) and insert (add) modes. In the **insert mode**, you insert new characters at the insertion point. Any existing characters are moved to make space for the new text. In **type-over mode**, any existing text is replaced the characters you type. You will try this yourself in a later lesson.

Home

This key moves the cursor to the beginning of the current line of type in a word processor or the beginning of a row in a spreadsheet. It performs essentially this same function in most software. In some cases, it is used in conjunction with the Control key to also move to the very beginning of a document.

End

This key is the opposite of the home key. It moves the cursor to the end of the line of type or the end of a row. It too can be combined with the Control key to move to the end of a document.

Delete or Del

This key is often confused with the backspace key, because it performs a similar, though opposite, action. The Delete key removes the character directly over or to the right of the cursor. (The backspace key removes the character to the left of the cursor.)

PgUp

The Page Up key moves the cursor "up" one full screen. If there is only one page, the cursor will move to the top of the page.

PgDn

The Page Down key moves the cursor "down" one full screen. If there is only one page, the cursor will move to the bottom of the page.

The Up Arrow Key (↑)

The Up Arrow key moves the cursor up one line or row. It will not move the cursor beyond the first line of a document.

The Down Arrow Key (↓)

The Down Arrow key moves the cursor down one line or row, but will not move the cursor beyond the end of the document.

The Left Arrow Key (←)

The Left Arrow key moves the cursor one character to the left. Be sure you find the left arrow key and not the backspace key which is sometimes marked with a left pointing arrow.

The Right Arrow Key (→)

The Right Arrow key moves the cursor one character to the right.

Print Screen

This key is a holdover from the past when it was used to print text and command line displays to the system printer. The Print Screen key is now used to capture a graphic copy of the current screen and place it on the Windows 95 Clipboard, a feature we will study in Lesson 3. Most software packages have print functions built into them, so it is unlikely that you would ever use this key to print a document or file.

Scroll Lock

The Scroll Lock key is used to stop the display from changing or "scrolling." As a computer beginner, you should have little or no use for this key, especially when working in the Windows 95 environment. Although a keyboard indicator light may come on, Windows 95 ignores this key. Should you press it by mistake, press it again to turn off the indicator light.

The Pause/Break key

This Pause/Break key is used with some software to pause or stop the action of the program. In the Windows 95 environment, this key is mostly ignored. Should a program activate it, you will be instructed on its use.

Number Pad

☞   Continue locating keys on the keyboard:

The number pad, located on the right side of the keyboard, is used for entering large volumes of numbers, see Figure 2-5. The numbers in the alphabetic or typewriter keys are very awkward to use for this purpose. The number pad resembles the ten-key entry pad found on many adding machines. It even contains the keys that are used to enter numeric functions (/ * - and +) into spreadsheets and similar programs, as well as an Enter key.

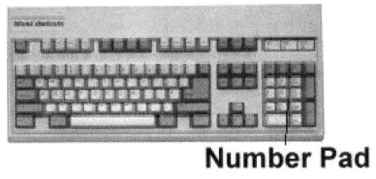

Number Pad

Figure 2-5: The Keyboard Number Pad

When a keyboard does not include the cursor control key section, the number pad can also be used as the cursor control keyboard. It is toggled out of number mode with the Num Lock key.

Num Lock

This key toggles the number pad between number mode and cursor control. An indicator light is lighted when the number pad is in number mode. Most computers start up the keyboard with the number p[ad in number mode.

Many of the cursor and mode control keys (insert, delete, the arrow keys, etc.) have duplicates on the number keypad. with the Num Lock key off, the "0/Ins" key can be used to toggle between insert and type-over modes. With the Num Lock key toggled on, this key is then a 0 (zero) key. You should always verify the number pad's mode before you use it by checking the Num Lock indicator light.

Key Repeat

When pressing keys, remember to touch them lightly and only once. Most computer keyboards now come with a feature called key repeat. If you hold the key down, the computer will continue to generate the keystroke signal and insert (or delete) as many characters as it has received signals, which may not be what you wanted to do. If you are in insert mode, eventually the computer will sound its alarm to warn you that you have filled up the input holding area and that no more keystrokes are being accepted.

Things to Remember

TERMS

Define and explain each of the following key types or terms:

Alt	End
arrow keys	Enter
backspace	Esc
Caps Lock	function keys
Control	Home
cursor	hot-key
Delete	Insert/Ins

key repeat

Num Lock

Pg Dn

Pg Up

Print Screen

Shift

Tab

toggle key

LESSON 3
FLOPPY DISKS

A floppy disk (Figure 3-1) is a portable, removable permanent storage media that is also called a floppy disk, a micro-disk, or simply a disk. Floppy disks are recorded and read by a floppy disk drive usually located in the system unit of a PC. Virtually every PC sold today has at least one floppy disk drive.

The primary benefit of the floppy disk is its convenience. Your documents can be stored on a floppy disk and taken with you, instead of staying on the computer's hard disk. This allows you to work on any computer that has the software you used to create the document.

Figure 3-1: Floppy disks, a.k.a. diskettes

Floppy disks are generally pre-formatted and ready for use when you buy them anymore, but all floppy disks must be formatted for use on a PC, a process called **formatting** (there's Mr. Obvious again). Formatting a disk creates a kind of street map of the floppy disk and as well as a list of the good and bad parts of the floppy disk.

Types and Styles of Floppy disks

Although there are several types and styles of floppy disks you can use, most of today's computers only support the 3.5-inch floppy disk shown in Figure 3-2. Some PCs still accept a 5.25-inch floppy disk, also included in Figure 3-2, although this size of floppy disk is generally considered obsolete.

Floppy disks have a range of storage capacities, indicated with a set of identifying initials. These initials represent how much data can be stored on a floppy disk and with which kind of floppy disk hardware it should be used.

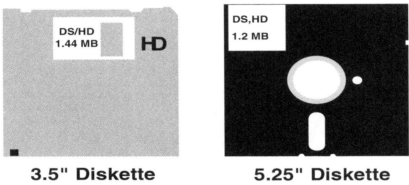

Figure 3-2: 3.5-inch and 5.25-inch floppy disks (obviously not to scale)

The following sections list the commonly used numbers, types and initials on floppy disks:

Size

As stated above, the 3.5-inch floppy disk is now the general standard size. There are some of the older 5.25-inch floppy disks still around, but they are disappearing fast. Some of the newer digital cameras use a 2.5-inch floppy disk, but even these are giving way to the standard 3.5-inch disk.

Sides

The number of sides of the physical media on which your data is recorded is indicated by a set of initials usually found on the floppy disk label.

SS   Single-Sided

Data is stored on only one side of the disk.

DS   Double-Sided

Data is stored on both sides of the disk.

Density

A pair of initials (either DD or HD) is used to indicate the amount of data or characters that can be stored on the floppy disk and the type of floppy disk drive needed to read and write the floppy disk. There two storage densities commonly in used: Double Density and High Density.

DD   Double Density

This floppy disk type can store from 360,000 to 720,000 characters.

HD   High Density

This floppy disk type can store from 1.2 million to 1.4 million characters.

Double density, also called "low" density, floppy disks are indicated by the initials "DD" on the floppy disk box, label, or paper jacket. High density floppy disks carry the initials "HD" in the same places. See Figure 3-2 for an example of where these initials are placed on the disk.

Formatting

It is possible to purchase floppy disks already formatted, and most of them now come that way. Formatted floppy disks have the term "formatted" on the floppy disk label, box, and dust jacket.

Labels

Not all floppy disks have a manufacturer's label. Some are bought in bulk and come very plain. If your floppy disk does not have a label indicating its size or type, ask your instructor or laboratory monitor for help in finding out its type.

Using the right floppy disk

It is important that you use the appropriate disk for the floppy disk drive on your computer. Floppy disk drives are designed to support a particular type and density of media. In some cases, a floppy disk drive will support a floppy disk with a lower density, but a lower density floppy disk drive cannot read a floppy disk formatted with a higher density. This is assuming you understand that a 3.5" floppy disk will never work in a 5.25" floppy disk drive, and vice versa. Nearly all 3.5-inch floppy disk drives included on newer computers are high-density drives. If you have trouble using your floppy disk with a computer, seek assistance. It may not be that your floppy disk's bad; it may just be on the wrong computer. More on this in the next lesson.

Protecting Your Floppy disks

Floppy disks are made of a round piece of coated Mylar plastic. The disk is coated with a material that can be magnetized and will stay magnetized unless it is erased or some foreign substance (such as a fingerprint, smoke particle, etc.) is placed on the disk surface. The disk is permanently sealed inside a protective plastic jacket. The plastic Mylar disk is very sensitive. Table 3-1 lists some of the things you should and should not do to insure your floppy disk is usable. There is nothing worse then losing all your data because your floppy disk becomes damaged.

DO	DON'T
Return your diskette to the protective envelope when not using it.	Never expose your diskette to extreme cold or hot or magnetic items.
Always insert your diskette slowly into the diskette drive taking care not to bend, crease or force it into the drive.	Never touch the exposed surfaces of the diskette or open the sliding cover of the diskette.
Always label the diskette by writing out the label before you put in on the diskette.	Never write directly on your diskette - the pen or pencil point may scar the diskette surface through the protective jacket
Always place the diskette in a protective box when carrying it.	Never place a diskette loose in your book or bag.

Table 3-1. Floppy disks Do's and Dont's

Things to Remember

☞ In the table below, first record the size, density, and sides specification of the floppy disk drive on the computer you will be using. Your instructor or the lab monitor should be able to give you this information. Then go to your school bookstore or to a local computer supply store and identify as many different floppy disk types as you can find. Enter the density, sides and size designations, and whether the floppy disk has a label or is already formatted, for each floppy disk type you find.

☞ Be sure to buy one. You'll need it later. Your instructor will tell you which type you'll need.

	Computer	Diskette #1	Diskette #2
Size			
Density			
Sides			
Label?			
Formatted?			

Terms

Explain or define each of the following terms relating to floppy disks.

Diskette

DD

DS

formatting

HD

label

size

sides

density

LESSON 4
DATA STORAGE

After you have spent what seems like eternity working on a document, it is only natural that you would want to save it for later reference or use. In this lesson, you earn the process used to save your work and review what the computer does to store your document.

As you learned in Lesson 2, while you are working on a document it is stored in the computer's memory. You should also remember that memory, a.k.a. RAM, is volatile, and should anything happen to the power, it could be erased in an instance, taking your hard work with it. Your documents should be save frequently to permanent storage - a disk.

Figure 4-1: Nothing is more frustrating than loosing a document in which you have invested a lot of time.

As you create documents on the computer, you should save your work on disk. Saving your work allows you to continue working at a later time or recover your work should something happen to the computer. Saving a document on your disk is similar to making a copy of the document and filing it away. Although most of the newer software packages have automatic save functions, the real responsibility for saving your work is on you. If you forget to save your document, it can be lost, right along with the time it took to create it. Okay, enough threats, we're here to learn about data storage, so let's get on with it.

Bits and Bytes

Regardless of what you may think or may have heard, the computer works quite simply. In fact, everything its does is based on sets of two opposite and unequal values: zero and one, true and false, yes and no, on and off, light and dark, go and stop, and so forth. This is because the computer is based on and relies very heavily on electricity and its properties.

Figure 4-2: A light bulb can be either "on" or "off"

Think of a switch that controls a light bulb like that in Figure 4-2. The switch is either on or off, and can never be both. This "either or" condition is also the basis for the computer's inner workings. The computer works on the principle that electricity can be only be in one of two states: on or off.

The computer is nothing more than a sophisticated electrical appliance. The early computer developers used many different types of storage devices to indicate or hold the computer's on's and off's. At first they used mechanical switches, then moved to the vacuum tube, and finally to the **transistor**, which is still in use today. These electronic components store a plus electrical charge (on) or a negative electrical charge (off).

These storage units store what is called a **binary digit**. The binary digit is generally known by its short name - bit (short for **bi**nary digit). A **bit** is stored in one of the electronic components that holds a plus or minus charge of electricity representing an on or off, plus or minus, or yes or no value.

The word **binary** means two values. It is also the name of a number system that contains only the two values zero and one. As you can see, a binary system works very well to represent the limits of electricity and the two values that the computer uses.

In spite of these developments, computer developers faced the problem that there are more than two characters in the English language. If English only had two letters, say A and B, then storing data would not be a problem. "On" could represent A and "off" could represent a B. Of course, this would mean we could only store words that have the letters A and B in them, and our vocabulary would need to be quite limited. Fortunately, or unfortunately, depending upon how you look at it, we do have a few more letters, numbers and characters to store.

Coding Schemes

By combining eight bits together in a grouping called a **byte**, it was found that the computer could store all of the single character numbers, letters and punctuation of the English language and then some. This was accomplished by developing a special code that assigned each letter, number, and character a unique pattern of on and off binary values.

Codes have been used throughout history to represent events and language. Paul Revere, of American Revolution fame, used a kind of binary code to indicate if trouble was brewing. Remember? One lantern burning meant one thing and two lanterns burning meant another. Two values, two meanings.

Samuel Morse used a similar approach in the code he developed for the telegraph. He used dots and dashes to create a pattern for each number, letter, and special character to be transmitted over the wires. For example, dot - dot - dot represents an "S" and dash - dash - dash represents an "O" and there were similar dot or dash combinations for each of the other letters as well.

The computer also uses a standard coding scheme which is used to store data. The coding scheme used in the computer is called the **American Standard Code for Information Interchange,** or **ASCII** (ask-ee) for short. The ASCII chart in Figure 4-3 contains samples ASCII characters and their binary code patterns.

As shown in Figure 4-3, ASCII code uses binary coding to represent its characters with a unique set of ones and zeros. Each letter, whether upper-case, lower-case, number, or special character has a unique eight bit (one byte) pattern of ones and zeros. When data is stored in memory or on your disk, each character is converted into this code and then stored in a single byte. When the data is read from memory or a disk, the coded characters are converted back into text, numbers, or special characters for display.

CHARACTER	ASCII BINARY CODES
A	0100 0001
B	0100 0010
C	0100 0011
D	0100 0100
E	0100 0101
F	0100 0110
G	0100 0111
A	0110 0001
B	0110 0010
C	0110 0011
D	0110 0100
E	0110 0101
F	0110 0110
G	0110 0111
0	0011 0000
1	0011 0001
2	0011 0010
3	0011 0011
4	0011 0100
5	0011 0101
6	0011 0110
Space	0010 0000
!	0010 0001
"	0010 0010
#	0010 0011
$	0010 0100
%	0010 0101
'	0010 0110
(	0010 0111
½	1010 1011
¼	1010 1100
¡	1010 1101
«	1010 1110
»	1010 1111

Figure 4-3: Sample ASCII Character Codes

Disks and Filenames

Now let's look at how your documents and files are stored and organized on the disk. In an earlier lesson, we talked about how a disk must be formatted before it could be used on the computer. But what actually happens during the formatting operation and why is it important?

Tracks and Sectors

Whether you are formatting a floppy disk or a hard disk, the process used by the computer is the same. The computer first divides the disk into **sectors** and **tracks**, which are used to later to help place and locate files on the disk.

Tracks and sectors are much like the streets and avenues in a city. One way to think of them is that tracks are like the main thoroughfares and sectors the cross-streets. One other comparison to city streets is how buildings are assigned numbers for easy lookup and reference. If buildings and houses didn't have addresses, we would have to search up and down every street until we found the right one. To avoid this same problem, the computer divides the disk into the logical divisions for referencing.

As we said earlier, the disk is divided into logical divisions called tracks and sectors during formatting. These divisions play an important role in the placement of your data on the disk. Tracks and sectors provide an easy way for the computer to find locations to place new files or find old files.

The tracks on a disk are similar to the tracks on a recording tape. Your favorite music tape is divided into parallel sections that run the entire length of the tape. The music on one side of the tape is recorded on one set of tracks. Another set of tracks is used for the music on the other side of the tape. The music tape was formatted for this purpose.

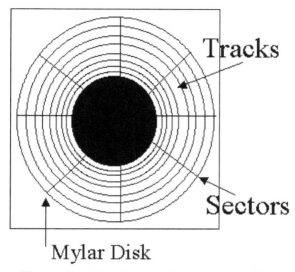

Figure 4-4: Tracks and Sectors on a Disk.

As illustrated in Figure 4-4, floppy disks are divided into 40 to 80 tracks depending on the disk, its density, and the type of disk drive. The hard disk is also divided into tracks. The number of tracks on the hard disk depends on the amount of storage space available and the particular technology in use. Tracks on a disk run concentrically (side-by-side) around the disk starting with track zero (the first track) near the center hub and ending near the outside edge. However, tracks on a disk are not like those of a phonograph record (surely you remember vinyl records!). One track is not connected to another; each track is continuous.

The disk is also divided into sectors. Sectors are logical divisions of the disk that resemble slices of a pie. Where they cross each track, it is divided into a segment that can store 512 characters. This creates a pattern on the disk that resembles the intersecting streets mentioned above. Each intersection of a sector and a track is an addressable point on the disk.

The address created at the intersection of a track and sector is used as a starting point for writing a file to the disk. Using an intersection as a reference point is much like locating a house in a city by using the names of the cross streets. For example, your data could be written on the disk at the intersection of the 28th track and the 7th sector, just like you might live at the corner of 28th Street and 7th Avenue.

File Allocation Table

The computer maintains a record of where your files are placed on the disk in a special table, called the **File Allocation Table,** or the FAT (pronounced f, a, t). The FAT is an index that enables the computer to find your data when you want to use it. The FAT is created when your disk is formatted and a list of all of the available addresses is entered into it. Each time you store a file to your disk, the address of its location is recorded along with the file name you assign to the file.

The FAT works much like the index in the lobby of a large building. The index lists all of the tenants of the building in alphabetical order, showing which suite each tenant occupies. In a similar way, the computer keeps track of your data by its name and at which track and sector location it was stored.

Files and Filenames

Data is stored on a disk in a file. A **file** contains all the characters you have entered and saved. A file is stored as a separate entity on the disk. In order to find your file later, you must assign it a unique name, which is used along with the file's address on the disk to create its entry in the FAT.

Before Windows 95, filenames were limited to 8 characters. This sometimes presented a real challenge in creating a meaningful and unique name. Windows 95 allows you to use what are called **long file names**. A filename must have at least one character but not more than 255 characters, more than enough to give the file a unique and meaningful name. The filename may contain spaces, but should not include a backward slash (\), forward slash (/)or period (.). Other than these simple rules, just about any name will work. Should you accidentally use a forbidden character in your filename, Windows 95 will display an error message.

For example, to name a file containing a memo regarding a employee's pay increase, we could name it "Ron's Raise Request to Connie.DOC" Since, this name conforms to the rules described above, it is a good filename and can be used. The name "Ron/Memo: Whining about a raise\Connie.TXT" is an invalid name because it contains illegal characters.

Filename Extensions

Windows and Microsoft Office automatically assign a file extension to each file written to the disk. The filename extension is attached to a filename to indicate the file's contents or type. The extension is not required, but if used, it must be between one and four characters in length.

The file extension indicates the type of data in the file or the software package that created it. It can also be used just to extend the filename for better meaning. In the sample filenames used above, the ".DOC" extension indicates that the file is a Microsoft Word document.

MS/DOS and Windows 95 both have files with file extensions already assigned. Each of these extensions has a certain meaning, as shown in the following table.

Extension	Meaning
.BAT	Batch file
.COM	MS/DOS Command
.DAT	Data file
.DLL	Dynamic Link Library
.EXE	Executable program
.HLP	Help file
.INI	Initialization code file
.SYS	MS/DOS or Windows system file
.TMP	Temporary file

Extensions are added to filenames with a period or, as us computer geeks call it, a dot. The dot is kind of like a trailer hitch that holds the extension to the filename. If you choose not to have an extension, because they are optional, do not use the dot.

Windows 95 automatically adds an extension on filenames to indicate the type of document and to tie it to the application that created it. For example, the suffix ".DOC" is added to text documents created in Microsoft Word. Excel documents are indicated with the extension ".XLS" and ".PPT" is added to PowerPoint documents. Our filename from above would pick up an extension when saved as "Ron Whining About a Raise.DOC."

Long filenames can also be stored in a short form by older software or program that do not support the long filenames. Other programs just ignore the long name and create an abbreviation of it. For example, the long file name used above might be displayed as "RONWHI~1.DOC" by a program not supporting long names. Other files that have the same first six letters in their names would be numbered incrementally as "RONWHI~2.DOC", etc.

Filename Summary

Let's summarize what we've learned about filenames and their extensions.

- ❖ filenames can be from 1 to 255 characters in length

- ❖ filenames cannot contain periods, the backslash (\) or the forward slash (/) character

- ❖ filename extensions can be from 1 to 3 characters in length

- ❖ filename extensions are optional, but, if used, must be separated from the filename with a period (which is why you cannot use a period in the name)

- ❖ filename extensions cannot contain periods, spaces or the backslash (\) characters (for the same reasons you can't use them in filenames).

Things to Remember

☞ Using the ASCII Character Chart in the lesson, substitute the binary character coding for each of the following:

FACE

dog

BED

beg

TERMS

Define and explain each of the following terms:

ASCII

binary

binary digit

bit

byte

FAT

file

filename

formatting

long filename

sectors

tracks

LESSON 5
WINDOWS 95

User Interfaces

The personal computer requires its operator to provide commands and data to it so that it can complete its tasks. The operator - you, the user - must tell the computer what you wish it to do and then input the data it needs. Your interaction with the computer is carried out through its **user interface**. The user interface accepts your commands and data and interprets them into actions and results.

There are two basic types of user interfaces: the character-based command interface and the graphical user interface.

Character/command interface

Before Windows, the user interacted with the computer by entering text commands at a command prompt, like the one shown in Figure 5-1.

$$\mathbf{C:\backslash>\_}$$

Figure 5-1: The DOS Command Line

Figure 5-1 is an example of the user interface of the **Disk Operating System** or **DOS**. An **operating system** is software that provides the user interface and interprets the commands and data entered. DOS systems, such as **MS/DOS** from the Microsoft Corporation and **PC/DOS** from the IBM Corporation, helped popularize the computer by making the computer accessible to every user in the early days of PCs.

The good news to early PC users was that DOS included a set of commands to help the user manage the computer hardware and to execute programs. These commands included FORMAT, TREE, and DATE, which respectively would format a disk, display a disk's files and structure, and display the system date. The bad news from DOS was that the user had to remember or look-up the commands for the actions desired and enter them at the command prompt. This was considered to be a very user-unfriendly interface.

Graphical User interface

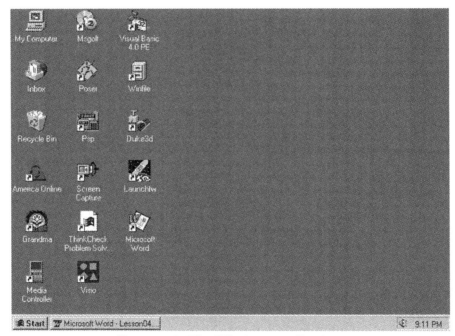

Figure 5-2: The Windows 95 Desktop

In effect, the graphical user interfaces of the Macintosh computer and the Windows operating system have replaced the command line interface of DOS. The **graphical user interface** (**GUI** - pronounced "gooey") uses graphic images to start actions on the computer instead of text commands. GUI images, called icons, provide graphic symbols that represent the commands and software choices are displayed on the monitor for the user's choice, see Figure 5-2. This results in a user friendly environment for the user who no longer needs to remember command words to perform tasks on the computer.

As illustrated in Figure 5-3, icons on the Windows Desktop represent applications, files, and shortcuts to other processes.

Figure 5-3: Icons on the Windows Desktop

The Mouse

Icons on the Windows desktop are selected and manipulated by a mouse. The mouse is a type of pointing device that allows the user to freely move an on-screen pointer around the display to highlight, select, or move icons and other graphical objects as desired by the user.

The mouse, shown in Figure 5-4, is operated by the user's hand. The user places their hand over the mouse and rolls it around on its mouse pad. The mouse rolls about on a protruding ball located on its underside. Sensors in the mouse detect the movement of the ball and the movement and direction of the mouse is translated into movement and position of the pointer on the screen.

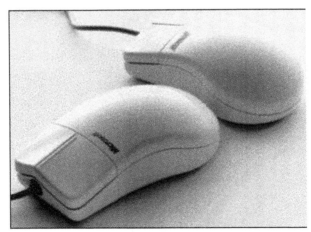

Figure 5-4: The Microsoft Mouse

Figure 5-5 illustrates the parts of the common two-button mouse. Each button is used differently, depending on the software, but typically the left-button is used to select an item or launch a process, and the right-button is used to display additional menu options. The left-button is the default action button on the mouse, but the right-button can be assigned as the default action button through the Windows Control Panel. If you are left-handed, check with your instructor to have this done.

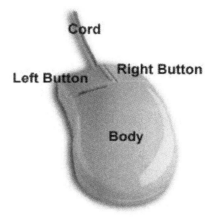

Figure 5-5: Mouse Anatomy

The GUI Environment

The GUI environment has become the PC interface standard largely because of the mouse. The mouse allows everyone to intuitively begin using a computer without needing to know any of the commands and filenames necessary in the past. The user indicates which actions are desired merely by moving the mouse and clicking its buttons This action becomes second-nature after a short amount of practice.

Mouse Commands

The mouse movements and buttons can be combined to create actions, each with a unique meaning to most software. The most common action is to simply place the on-screen pointer on an icon. Other actions include click, double-click, select, and drag and drop (see Figure 5-6). Each of these actions is used to accomplish a separate function. You will use these actions throughout this book, so it is important that you become familiar with the action, function and feel of each.

Figure 5-6 lists many of the commonly used mouse actions along with the mouse, hand, and button activities for each action. For example, to start a software program requires you to "point" the mouse pointer at the icon of the item you wish to start, and "double-click" the left mouse button. This action results in starting the software program. To "point" at an object, you merely move the mouse with your hand until the on-screen pointer is pointing to it. Pointing to an item will not cause a change to take place, other than the pointer is over the icon. "Double-click"-ing involves pressing the mouse button two times very quickly while pointing at the item. This is the signal that indicates to Windows 95 that you wish to run the program associated with the active icon.

ACTIONS	ACTIVITIES	RESULTS
Point	Move mouse with hand	Indicates the item on which action will be taken
Click	Press the mouse button once	Selects the point item
Double-Click	Press the mouse button twice rapidly	Starts the item selected.
Drag and Drop	Point to an object. Press and hold the mouse button. Point to new location and release the button	Picks-up an item and carries it to a new location.
Select	Press the mouse button once	See Click
Select Range	Click on the first item and while holding down the shift key, click on the last item in the range.	Selects a range of adjacent items
Select Random	Click on each item to be selected while holding down the Ctrl key.	Selects non-adjacent or random items

Figure 5-6: Common Mouse actions, activities and results

Now you try some of these actions:

☞ It is likely that your computer opens Windows when it starts up. If not, your instructor or lab monitor can provide you with instructions on how to start the Windows program.

🖰 Place your hand on the mouse so that the body of the mouse is in your palm and the heel of your hand rests on the surface right behind the mouse. The mouse should be on a mouse pad - a foam rubber pad with a cloth or plastic surface. Your hand should rest on the mouse pad. Your pointer finger should rest on the left button (right button for left-handed settings) and your index finger should rest on the right button (left for left-handed).

☞ Now find the pointer on the screen. In most installations, it will appear as an arrow pointing up to the left like the one in the Figure 5-7.

Figure 5-7: The Screen Pointer

🖰 Now, while looking at the display and not your hand, begin moving your hand slowly. Do you see the arrow on the screen moving? As you move your hand, the arrow should move around the screen accordingly. When you move the mouse away from your body, the screen pointer will move toward the top of the screen. When you move the mouse toward your body, the screen pointer will move toward the bottom of the display. Move your hand left, the pointer moves left. Move your hand right, the pointer moves right. Move your hand in a circle, guess what? You don't usually need to move your hand very far to move the screen pointer over most of the Windows desktop.

🖱 Continue practicing until you feel comfortable with your hand and eye coordination while using the mouse.

🖱 Pick out some objects on the Windows desktop and move the pointer to point to them. Don't use the buttons yet. If you do click a button and start an application by accident, point to the "X" button in the upper right corner of the window and click the mouse button again to close whatever you opened.

After you have become more comfortable with the mouse unit and the screen pointer, move ahead to the next part of this lesson.

Windows 95 Desktop

The startup screen, the Windows 95 **Desktop**, is unique to the computer or to the laboratory setup. Although there may be some local differences, your display should resemble the one shown in Figure 5-8.

The opening display is meant to resemble the top of your desk where you would place any tools needed to do your job and have them handy until they are needed. The Windows Desktop should be thought of as a collection of your frequently used tools placed on your desk ready for use.

Figure 5-8: Windows Desktop

Icons

There are two types of icons found on the desktop: built-in icons, such as My Computer and Recycle Bin, and frequently-used applications added by the user or system manager. In addition to program icons, Windows 95 also supports folders on the desktop. Icons, like My Computer, Explorer, and others allow you to open or start programs or other menus. The folder icon, like that shown in Figure 5-9, provides access to file directories and groups of data files or documents.

Figure 5-9. A Folder on the Desktop

Should you need a document or information, you would open a file folder to get it. As shown in Figure 23, the device used to store a document or other files in Windows 95 is the folder. Each folder has its own icon.

☞   Study the Windows 95 Desktop display looking for the Taskbar. The Taskbar is normally located along the bottom of the display and should resemble the Taskbar shown in Figure 5-10.

Figure 5-10: Windows Taskbar

Start button and taskbar

At the bottom of your screen is a solid gray bar called the **Taskbar**. At its left end, the taskbar contains the **Start** button, which you can use to quickly start a program, find a file, or change the desktop and taskbar settings. It's also the fastest way to get Help.

Figure 5-11: Windows 95 Taskbar Start Button

Each time you start a program, or open a document or a window, a button is added to the taskbar. As you open more applications, folders, or documents, more buttons are added to the taskbar. These buttons can be used to quickly switch between the open windows. As you close these windows, the buttons are removed.

Figure 5-12: Windows 95 Taskbar with Buttons for Open Windows

Launching an Application

Your first lesson in starting a program will be to open and use the Notepad utility program.

☝ Using the mouse, point to the Start button and click it. This will display the Start Menu, shown in Figure 5-13.

Figure 5-13: The Windows 95 Start menu

The Windows 95 **Start Menu** includes selections to:

❖ list the programs available for use on the computer

❖ list the documents most recently created or edited

❖ manage the desktop and taskbar settings

❖ help you find a file or program fast

❖ get help from the Windows 95 Help system

❖ help you run a program not included on the desktop or program list

❖ shut down or restart Windows 95 and your PC

You may add other selections as needed to customize the Desktop to your particular needs. However, in an office or school setting, the Desktop is often managed from a central source to ensure each user has access to all of the programs and features on the computer.

If the Start Menu has closed, click the start button again to display it. Point to the Programs … selection to display the Program Menu (see Figure 5-14) will display.

The **Program Menu**, an example in shown in Figure 5-14, lists group and single program selections that are available. The program menu you display may not have as many choices or even the same choices as that in Figure 5-14, or it may have more. The Program Menu is unique to the individual computer or network. Group program selections, the ones with the arrows pointing to the right, display other menus with choices for a group of related programs.

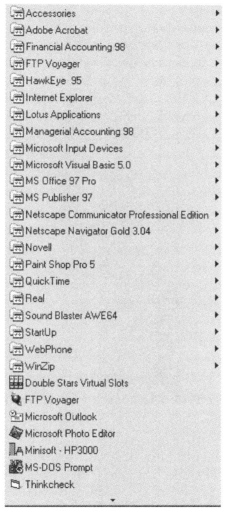

Accessories
Adobe Acrobat
Financial Accounting 98
FTP Voyager
HawkEye 95
Internet Explorer
Lotus Applications
Managerial Accounting 98
Microsoft Input Devices
Microsoft Visual Basic 5.0
MS Office 97 Pro
MS Publisher 97
Netscape Communicator Professional Edition
Netscape Navigator Gold 3.04
Novell
Paint Shop Pro 5
QuickTime
Real
Sound Blaster AWE64
StartUp
WebPhone
WinZip
Double Stars Virtual Slots
FTP Voyager
Microsoft Outlook
Microsoft Photo Editor
Minisoft - HP3000
MS-DOS Prompt
Thinkcheck

Figure 5-14: The Windows 95 Program Menu

With the Program Menu displayed, hold down the mouse button and slide it up the menu to point to the Accessories selection and released the mouse button. This should cause the menu shown in Figure 5-15 to appear.

Accessories Group

The Accessories menu shown in Figure 5-15 includes programs to assist you with commonly performed activities and other Windows tasks. Remember, Windows menus are often different from computer to computer, so if your menus differ from any the menu shown in the figures, it isn't because you've done anything wrong. However, if you suspect that something may be wrong, contact your instructor or lab monitor.

Figure 5-15: The Accessories Group Menu

🖱 With the Accessories menu displayed, hold down the mouse button and slide the pointer to the Notepad selection and release the button. The Notepad utility, a text editor, should open a new Notepad window, like the one in Figure 5-16.

Figure 5-16: A new Notepad window

If the Notepad program is now running, you have completed the steps correctly.

✍ If the Notepad window is not open on your desktop, go back and repeat the steps until you are successful. There is no telling just what may have gone wrong; a variety of things could have happened. The most likely problem is that you did not hold down the mouse button until the Notepad program was selected.

✍ If a window for another program is open on the desktop, you probably released the mouse button too soon. If so, click on the X button in the extreme right corner of this new window to close it, and click on the Start button to begin again. If after trying again, you are still not able to open the Notepad, ask your instructor or lab monitor for assistance.

Notepad

The Notepad program is a very simple text editing tool that you can use for text reading and writing purposes. For now we will use it only to demonstrate some of the other features of Windows 95 programs.

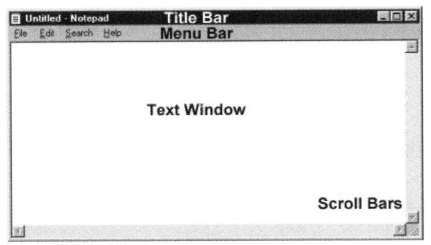

Figure 5-17: Notepad Window Elements

Beneath the Title Bar, the darkly colored bar (usually blue) at the top of the window, is Notepad's menu bar. Notepad has four menu selections: File, Edit, Search, and Help. Locate the menu bar.

🖑 Click on each Menu bar choice to display its contents.

As you work with Windows 95 programs, you will find that the menu bars are basically the same. Some may have more or fewer choices, but the sequence of the menu choices on the bar will fairly constant. This helps you by eliminating the need for you to memorize a different set of menu choices for each application.

Window Control Buttons

Figure 5-18: Window Control Buttons

In the upper right corner of the Notepad window are three buttons, illustrated in Figure 5-18. These buttons are used to control the window's size and to close it. The leftmost button reduces the window down to a button on the taskbar. This button is used to **minimize** the window. After you have done this, the minimize button changes to a **restore** button. The restore button, see Figure 5-19, is used to reverse any resize action.

Figure 5-19: Minimize button changed to Restore button.

The center button is the **maximize** button that enlarges the window to fill the screen. After a window has been maximized, this button also changes to restore button.

The rightmost button is the close button, the one with the big "X." The close button closes the window and returns control to Windows 95. You will be asked if you wish to save any unsaved open documents before the window is closed.

☞ Experiment with the minimize, maximize, and restore buttons. When you have reached Window Control Button Master Operator status, this is you are satisfied that you know and understand their functions, click on the close button to close the Notepad window.

* * *

Congratulations! You have succeeded in starting a Windows 95 application. You've used the Start button, the Program menu, and the Accessories group to start a Windows program!

And you said you didn't do Windows!

My Computer and Formatting a Disk

The **My Computer** window, see Figure 5-20, displays an icon for each of the storage devices on the computer, including a few group icons for the Control Panel, Printers and others.

Figure 5-20: Windows My Computer Window

The My Computer window is a built-in icon on the Windows 95 Desktop that Windows automatically includes on the desktop. As shown in Figure 5-21, the My Computer icon is normally located in the upper-left corner of the Windows 95 Desktop.

Figure 5-21: The My Computer Icon on the Windows Desktop

✍ If you have not already done so, close the Notepad application by clicking on its Close button. This should take you back to the Windows 95 desktop. Close any other applications running on the desktop as well. This should return you to the Desktop with the Taskbar empty, except for the Start button, of course.

✍ Double-click on the My Computer icon. Recall that double-clicking means to click the mouse button twice very quickly on an icon. If you are successful, the window shown in Figure 5-20 should appear. If you are having trouble, ask your instructor or lab monitor for assistance.

Formatting your disk

As mentioned in an earlier lesson, disks of all types must be formatted before the computer can use them. A formatted disk contains a "road map" of the usable and available areas on the disk, segmented into small sections of the disk that can be found quickly.

✍ Insert your disk into the appropriate floppy disk drive for your floppy disk.

✋ Insert your disk into the appropriate disk drive. It is likely that your computer has only one floppy disk drive, and it is also likely that it is a 3.5-inch drive. Make sure you have the right floppy disk for your computer. If you have the wrong size or type -stop, get the proper floppy disk, and continue. If you have the correct size, continue with the lesson.

Your disk drive is probably designated as **A:** (pronounced "A-colon"). If your computer has two floppy disk drives, you may need to ask your instructor or lab monitor to show you which drive is the A: drive. The second disk drive is likely designated as **B:**.

✋ With the My Computer group window open, find the icon for the A: drive. Figure 5-22 includes a sample of it. Click once on this icon to select it. Its image and words should darken which indicates that it is selected.

3½ Floppy (A:)

Figure 5-22: The A: Drive Icon on the My Computer Group Window

Now click the action button on the mouse (left button for right-handers; right button for left-handers). A shortcut menu, like that shown in Figure 5-23, should appear. Study the shortcut menu and take notice of the types of actions you can perform on your floppy disk. About half of the way down the menu list, you will find the selection for "Format ... ."

Figure 5-23: My Computer Shortcut Menu

Click on the Format choice to display a dialog box, like that shown in Figure 5-24.

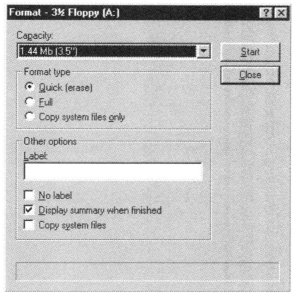

Figure 5-24. Format Disk Dialog Box

The dialog box shown in Figure 35 is used to format a floppy disk. The options available set the type of formatting to be done, the electronic label of the disk and whether or not a disk is a system disk or not.

As shown in Figure 5-24 there are two formatting choices: **quick (erase) formatting** and **full formatting**. The quick format option is used for formatted disks that may have old and unwanted files them. This option merely cleans the disk by erasing the files. New disks, the unsolicited disks you get in the mail, or disks that may have corrupted files on them, should be formatted with the full format option.

The system files option creates a disk that can be used to boot the computer should anything happen to the hard disk. This is a topic for a more advanced course.

　◌   Click on the "Full" option button. A black dot should appear in the button.

If you buy a new disk labeled "Formatted," it is probably ready for use on your computer. Even if your disk is pre-formatted, and you always plan to buy formatted disks in the future, you should still follow these instructions to format your disk. If is very likely that at some point in the future, you will want to refresh or erase a disk so it can be reused.

　◌   Click on the Label box. Enter up to eleven (11) characters of your name. Do not use punctuation characters (periods, commas, or the like) or either of the slash characters. You may use spaces between words. When finished, do **NOT** press the enter key. Instead press the Tab key to advance to the Start button or use the mouse to click the Start button.

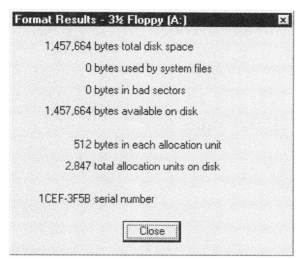

Figure 5-25: Formatted Disk Summary

As Windows 95 formats your disk, it displays a blue bar scale along the bottom of the dialog box to indicate the percentage of the disk that has been completed. Do not interrupt the formatting, because this is an "all or nothing" deal. If the formatting does not complete, the disk is not properly formatted and will not be usable by the computer.

When formatting is complete, a disk summary message box will display. As shown in Figure 5-25, it displays the total space on the disk, and the amount of usable disk available. Don't worry if there is some bad sectors on your disk, unless it is most of the disk space available. A few bad sectors are common.

Click the button marked "Close" or the Close button to close the message box. This will return you to the Format dialog box; close this box. You should return to the My Computer window. Close the My Computer Window and return to the Desktop.

You have now explored the fundamentals of starting and closing a program in Windows 95 and those used to format a disk for use on the computer. In the lessons ahead, you will use the floppy disk you have just formatted to save and retrieve your documents as you work in Microsoft Word.

Things to Remember

Terms
Define or explain each of the following terms:

> Accessories group
>
> Click
>
> Desktop
>
> DOS
>
> Double-click
>
> Drag and drop
>
> Formatting
>
> GUI
>
> Icon
>
> Maximize
>
> Minimize
>
> Mouse
>
> MS/DOS
>
> My Computer
>
> Notepad
>
> PC/DOS

Point

Program menu

Operating system

Screen pointer

Select

Select Random

Select Range

Start menu

Taskbar

User interface

LESSON 6
INTRODUCTION TO RESEARCH

Figure 6-1: Effective research is essential to a successful report.

One of the many benefits of learning to use the computer is that you can use it to create some very nice-looking documents. The computer and its software are powerful tools you can apply to the creation of impressive, eye-appealing letters, memo, reports, and other documents.

As mentioned earlier, the lessons in this book guide you through the creation of a research paper. The paper you create in this book is intended to be similar to one you might actually prepare for a class. By creating this paper you will learn to use the computer's hardware and software to produce the result you desire.

The computer, its software, or this book cannot do the fact-finding necessary for the content of your document. <u>You</u> must perform this step. Only you know what the paper is to say, what its objectives are, what its conclusions should be, and what facts should be included to support your conclusions. You must do the research.

Early Research

Although most research for a paper is done after the topic and thesis have been chosen, some research can precede them. Usually the topic of a paper is left for you to decide. When the topic of the paper is left for you to decide, it can be difficult to narrow an entire field of study into a single topic. This is especially true if you are choosing the report's topic early in a term when very little of the class has been covered.

Literature Search

One solution is to perform what is called a **literature search**. Searching through the school, community, or regional library or on the Internet or World Wide Web, you may find some information that interests you. This type of search looks to uncover as much material as possible on a subject without regard to limiting factors or search criteria constraints.

A literature search performs two services: it lets you see the amount of research material available on a subject; and it provides sources for information within the subject area. If very little material is available on a subject, you may wish to look for another subject or adjust the search topic. Likewise, if the sources of the material are limited to only one or two, this may not be enough perspective for your paper.

On the other hand, should you find a sufficient quantity of material and sources for the subject area, you can choose a report topic with some confidence that you have sufficient resources on which to draw in writing the report.

Some reports require a thesis statement and others do not. A thesis statement is an arguable statement of opinion that can be proven or refuted by invoking the comments, facts and judgments found in the research. Many scholars contend that whether or not a thesis statement is required in the paper, all research writing is based upon a thesis. For example, we could have stated the thesis of the research paper developed in this book as "Retirement planning must begin when people are 20-30 years of age." This statement can easily be argued, and very likely there are ample research materials available.

The thesis also identifies the topic of the report. Clearly, our topic is retirement planning.

Research Tools

Regardless of how you plan to do your research, the best place to start is your school, public, or regional library. This is an appropriate place to start because nearly all of the general information resources for the school or community are located there. Most also have access to the Internet and other on-line services to enhance your research beyond the holdings of the library.

The library contains information resources in all forms of technology as well. Your library most certainly has printed materials in books and periodicals, but it may also have some materials on microfilm or microfiche or stored on a computer hard disk. **Microfilm** and **microfiche** are rolls of film or cards that hold highly reduced images that are shown on a viewer which magnifies the stored image.

Your library may also have a collection of CD-ROMs that contain many types of reference information, see Figure 6-2. Because they can hold so much data, one CD-ROM disk can replace dozens of card catalog drawers. In addition, the CD-ROM usually is supported by search software that can perform searches for the author, title, subject, publisher, or any word contained in the material. CD-ROM drives use the same technology as your home CD player. There are single CD drives, multi-disk magazine drives, rotary or carousal drives and tower units also called "juke boxes."

Figure 6-2: An external CD-ROM drive

CDs can store a complete year of a magazine - pictures and all, entire years of newspapers, all of the books in print, or entire encyclopedia. Special systems have also been created to take advantage of the storage capacity to present multi-media reference materials, such as Microsoft's Encarta®.

In addition, the library may have computer-based on-line information available that can be searched to find references to magazines and other periodicals, books or statistical materials that can then be accessed physically or electronically to complete the research.

☞   Visit your school or public library and note each of the various types of research tools available for you to use in your research. Identify each tool, explain its use and the type of information it can provide.

Research Methods

There are a number of different approaches you can use to start your research. In general, the purpose of your early research is to take stock of the resources available for your paper. The list you generate from this step should contain enough information about each reference item so that you can later decide whether or not to use it in your paper. The information you collect should include the author's name, the title of the article, the book or the publication, the date of the material, a summary of its contents, its URL (Internet address), and how or where you found it.

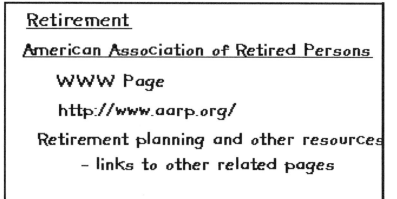

Figure 6-3. Early research creates an inventory of available sources

There are several standards that prescribe the form your early research should take. Some recommend using 3" X 5" index cards with each card holding the reference information for a single piece (see Figure 6-3). Another recommended approach is to create a list that looks like a bibliography in the making. There are other recommended methods as well. Many schools have research and report standards. Your instructor should be able to explain your school's standards, if any exist. You might also check with your school's writing lab or your English instructor.

The Internet & World Wide Web as Research Tools

As we stated earlier, the Internet and World Wide Web (the Web) are excellent resources for finding information on a wide range of topics and subjects. With literally millions of locations offering information on just about anything you can think of, there is sure to be at least a few sites to help you with information for your report. In this section, you will be introduced to how the Web can be used as a research tool.

For purposes of your research, the following section introduces you very briefly to the Internet and the World Wide Web and some of the specialized tools available - search engines (Figure 6-4). Later in the book, you will get a more in depth look at the Internet and the World Wide Web (WWW or "the Web").

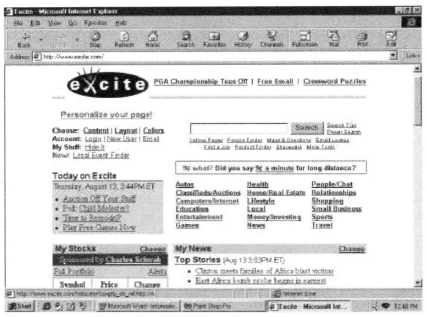

Figure 6-4: The Excite search engine

The research paper developed in this book is about "retirement planning." We have chosen this subject because it is a good generic topic that should be of interest to just about everyone, whether they realize it or not. In addition, a large amount of research materials are available on this and related subject areas. There are many magazines, books, pamphlets, Web sites, and other resources dedicated to this subject. In fact, if you were to expand your research to include personal interviews, there are professionals that specialize in retirement planning.

The following exercise has two purposes: to demonstrate the amount of material available by looking at only one source; and to introduce you to the use of electronic search tools. In this exercise, you will use a search engine to find on-line locations for information relating to retirement planning.

Your instructor or lab monitor should explain how to access a Web browser on your computer. A **browser** is a GUI used to display the specially formatted files and links used to create the image of the World Wide Web.

✍   Find the button or menu selection on your browser that displays its search page. It is normally labeled Search. Click it to open the search page of your browser. The Web page that displays should resemble that shown in Figure 6-5 below.

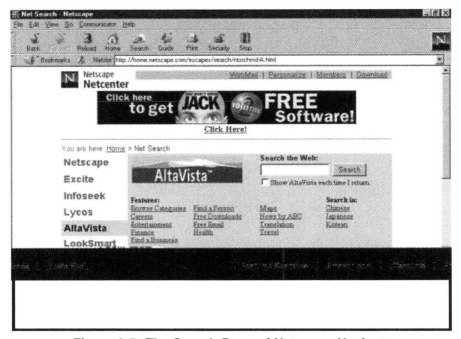

Figure 6-5: The Search Page of Netscape Navigator

Search engines search. (Mr. Obvious strikes again) Through a search engine you can locate sites anywhere in the world with information on a term, phrase, or subject. After searching its database, the search engine displays a list of qualifying sites for you to check. If the search has resulted in more than ten or twenty, the list will be divided up and displayed one page at a time. It is not unusual for some searches to find over a million or more qualifying sites, depending on the topic.

Select one of the search engines available by clicking on its icon or button.

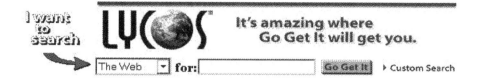

Figure 6-6: The Lycos Search Prompt

An empty text box, as illustrated above should be displayed like that in Figure 6-6.

🖑 Enter the words "retirement planning" (without the quote marks) and press the enter key or click on the Submit, Search, of Get It! button located at the right end or just below the text box.

In a remarkably short time, the search engine will respond a list of entries it found in its database that match, or are very close to, the search term you entered. In this case, the search criteria told the search engine to find Web sites that contained the phrase retirement planning. The references included in the list, illustrated in Figure 6-7, can be used to move or "jump" to the other Web pages listed. Each of the items listed contains a link or a reference to its location on the Web.

Figure 6-7: Retirement Planning search results

The list return has a link to the site as well as its title and a brief description of what you will find there, as shown in Figure 6-8.

1. RETIREMENT PLANNING SERVICES
[URL: wwwcpo.elan.af.mil/PALACE_COMPASS/EMPLOYEE/sld013.htm]
nbsp;
Last modified 7-Aug-97 - page size 1K

2. Retirement Planning - 1997 Federal Budget
[URL: www.acelink.com/fp-guide/retirement_5.html]
Ralph Moss Limited. 1997 Federal Budget...good common sense is re-established regarding pension plans! Today, the work force is more mobile than ever. A...
Last modified 4-Mar-97 - page size 15K - in English

3. Retirement Planning - An Attorney's Look at Tax Planning for the Small Busines
[URL: dev.abanet.org/cle/catalog/t96tps5.html]
American Bar Association Continuing Legal Education. An Attorney's Look at Tax Planning for the Small Business Owner, Rancher and Farmer Retirement...
Last modified 9-Oct-97 - page size 3K - in English

Figure 6-8: Search results

The list returned should contain a number of links to other Web sites which have met your search criteria. The links are usually underlined and shown in one of two colors: a dark color, such as dark blue and a lighter color, such as red. These colors indicate whether a link has been visited or not. In this example, the blue links have not been visited and the red links are sites that you have visited. This is a feature of the Web that helps prevent you visiting sites you have already seen. Clicking on any of the links causes the browser to access the referenced file from its host location and display it on your computer.

🖑 Click on one or two of the items included in the list returned by your search engine.

To determine if you can use the site in your research, you should read its summary or visit the site by clicking on its link. If the site is promising or you wish to visit it later, you should note its address for later reference. A Web site's address is called its **URL** which means **Uniform Resource Locator**. The URL is usually an Internet address in the form of:

http: //www.mycollege.edu/mypages/myfile.html

The above URL contains the type of file transfer that will be used to move the document to your computer, the Internet address of the computer that has the file, and the name of the file. **Http** is the abbreviation for **hypertext transfer protocol**, the standard transfer type used on the Web. Most Web pages are encoded in a hypertext language.

Bookmarks

Once you find a site you wish to visit again later without having to rerun the search engine, you can create what is called a **bookmark**. A bookmark captures the title and Internet address of a Web page and saves them in a list that you manage. This is sort of like creating an electronic note card for the site.

Figure 6-8: The Tool and Menu Bars of Netscape Navigator

As shown in Figure 6-8, the tool bar contains a button for Bookmarks Clicking on the bookmark button will display all existing bookmarks you have save and give you the option of adding another bookmark entry.

☜ Click on the Bookmark button and look at the bookmark list for your computer. Add a bookmark for one or more of the Web sites you found in your search. Re-examine the bookmark list. Is your new bookmark listed?

Other Research Tools

The Internet is just one of the tools you can use to do your research. Some users believe the Internet and Web are a good first step for performing research. The Internet, by its very nature, is generally up-to-date with new resources being added every minute of every day. Others believe it should be the final step in your research and used to verify or supplement your print material research. However, and whenever, you use it, please remember that it will be quite some time before all of the references and information you need can be found on the Internet. While a lot of information is available on the Internet today, and more is available every day, a great deal of information is still available only through a search of catalogs, lists, CDs, and the like. And just because something is on the Internet does not give it better credibility over any other information source - it may just be more current.

One other caution about the Internet and Web - Just because information is on the Internet does not make it credible. With the tools that are available to help you publish to the Web, anyone, and we mean anyone, is a publisher and can post information on the Web regardless of its source, content, and truthfulness. So like much else in the world - buyer beware!

☞ Visit the library and find at least 15 potential information sources on a topic related to retirement planning. At least three of the sources should be on the Internet, but not more than six. Include in your references, the title of the source and where it can be found.

Note to the student

The research paper built in these lessons is not complete; parts were omitted to try to save a few trees during printing.

Things to Remember

Answer each of the following questions regarding Lesson 6.

☞   Investigate whether Internet service is available to you locally or nearby.

  ❖   What are the costs of using this service?

  ❖   Search for retirement planning information using different search engines. Did you get the same results with each?

  ❖   When, how and why should the Internet and the Web be used in research?

Terms

Define, identify, or explain each of the following terms

> bookmark
>
> browser
>
> CD-ROM
>
> ftp
>
> http
>
> Internet
>
> link
>
> literature search

microfiche

microfilm

search engine

thesis

topic

URL

World Wide Web

SECTION 2
WORD PROCESSING WITH WORD 97

Word Processing

Word Processing software is used to create, edit, format, and print documents. Word processing automates many actions we would perform manually on a typewriter. Unlike the typewriter, computer word processing software has the ability to store a document for future use. You can retrieve a document that has been stored, make changes to it, and store the revised copy. The document can be checked for spelling and grammar errors using features of the software. The margins and line spacing can be changed simply and easily. The document you have created can be edited without retyping the whole document the way you would on a typewriter.

When typing continuously in a word processor, the text is automatically carried to the next line when a word does not fit at the end of the current line. This feature is called word wrap. The word processing software also keeps track of how many lines of text will fit on a page according to the margins that have been set. When the page is full the software will start a new page.

As you type characters on the screen, you are entering data. Data are raw facts, letters, numbers, and symbols that are processed by the computer. When data is processed and made meaningful through human interpretation it becomes information.

Word Defaults

When you enter a word processing program some initial, built in settings automatically come up. These initial settings are called default settings. Defaults are settings that are available automatically without any action on your part. Default settings allow you to begin typing without worrying about setting up a format for your document. Always check to see what the default settings are in any word processing package you are using. Each word processing software package's defaults are different.

The following are some of the Word 97 for Windows 95 default settings:

❖   The text that you type is single-spaced.

❖   The left and right margins are set 1.25 inches from the sides of the page.

❖   The tabs are preset every ½ inch.

❖   The top and bottom margins are automatically set at 1 inch; the printer will add these.

❖   The word-wrap feature is On. You don't need to press Return or Enter at the end of each line.

❖   Insert mode is on. This means that if you wish to type more text into an existing document, any text after the cursor (insertion line) will be pushed ahead as you type and the new text will be inserted into the document.

❖   The Justification feature is set at Left justify. This means that the text you type will be even at the left margin but uneven (like text typed on a typewriter) on the right side margin.

❖   The font (style of the characters) is Times New Roman.

❖   The point size is 10. A character with a point size of ten is about 10/72 of an inch in height.

❖ When a page is full of text, the program will automatically put a soft page break in the document. The soft page break appears as a dotted line across the screen.

❖ Headers and footers appear within the top and bottom margins of a document. They appear ½ inch from the paper's edge.

Cursor movement keys

The following is a quick review of the cursor movement keys, you were first introduced to in Lesson 2:

˃	Previous line
fl	Next line
Ctrl + ˃	Previous paragraph
Ctrl + fl	Next paragraph
˂	Previous character
fi	Next character
Ctrl + ˂	Previous word
Ctrl + fi	Next word
Home	Beginning of line
End	End of line
Ctrl + Home	Beginning of document
Ctrl + End	End of document
PgUp	Show previous screen
PgDn	Show next screen
Backspace	deletes the character to the left of the cursor (insertion line)
Delete	deletes the character to the right of the cursor (insertion line)

MLA Format

The following points describe the style guide of the MLA (Modern Language Association) standard for documents. The MLA style is the guideline used for the lessons you will perform throughout this book.

❖ 1 inch top and bottom margins.

❖ 1 inch left and right margins.

❖ Tabs set every ½ inch.

❖ Line spacing is double.

❖ Page numbers are ½ inch from the top margin in the upper right-hand corner of each page, suppressed on the first page. The page number is preceded by the writers last name typed all in capital letters and followed by the page number.

❖ On the first page of your document, place your name and course information in a block at the left margin.

❖ Center the title two double-spaces below your name and course information.

❖ In the body of the paper, place author references in parentheses with page numbers where the reference information is located.

❖ Create a Works Cited page. This contains the bibliographical references used in the paper. Place the works cited information on a separate numbered page. List the works alphabetically by each author's last name. Center the title **Works Cited**. Begin the first line of each work cited at the left margin: indent all subsequent lines of the same reference ½ inch from the left margin.

LESSON 7
STARTING WORD 97

Throughout the lessons dealing in Word 97 any time you are told point and click, you are expected to use the mouse. If you need to use the menu it will be indicated.

Reminder: The symbol ⬚ indicates that some action should be taken:

* ❖ use of the mouse

* ❖ typing characters

* ❖ menu selections

Starting Word

Check with your instructor on how to start Word on your system. If the steps are different than the steps given below, write them down in your notes for future reference.

⬚ Click on the **Start** button

⬚ Move the mouse pointer up to **Programs** and Click

⬚ Move the pointer to the right and highlight **Microsoft Office 97**

⬚ Move the pointer to the right and highlight **Microsoft Word**

The desktop should now look something like this (remember, every desktop can be unique and yours most likely does not look exactly like this one):

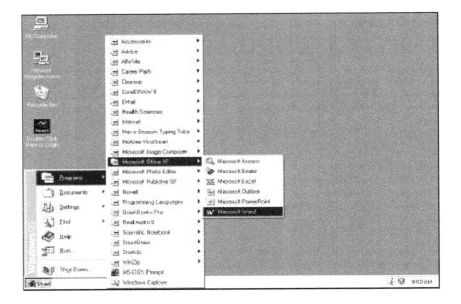

🖰 Click on **Microsoft Word 97**

You are now in Microsoft Word 97 and ready to work on your document. First, let's get oriented to the Word screen.

The elements of the Word 97 window are explained in the following table and illustrated in the graphic that follows:

Application window	The larger of the two Word windows, used to provide communication between the user and the Word program
Document window	The smaller or inner window, used to create and edit the active Word document
Title Bar	Displays the name of the Word application and the document name
Menu Bar	Displays the Word menu options. (Located below the title bar)
Tool Bar	Contains buttons providing quick access to frequently used word commands and utilities
Ruler	Provides page measurements and is used to change margins, paragraph tabs, and indents (located below the tool bars)

Scroll Bars	Displays different portions of the active document. Located along the bottom and right side of the document window
Status Bar	Displays the following information: page number, section number, number of pages in the document, the position of the insertion point, line number, and column number (located at the bottom of the screen)
Insertion line	A vertical bar indicating your current location, cursor position
I-beam	Used as a pointer (mouse pointer) to select text or position the insertion line

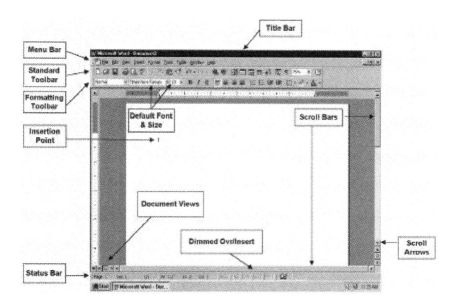

Toolbars

Word 97 has two fundamental toolbars: the standard toolbar and the formatting toolbar. A toolbar is an arrangement of icons that can be used to access or start features within the Word application.

Standard toolbar

Standard toolbar. The Standard toolbar contains the buttons most commonly used during document creation, file handling, and printing.

Formatting toolbar

Formatting toolbar. The Formatting toolbar contains buttons used for formatting fonts, setting text alignment, applying numbering or bullets, indents, and borders.

Entering Text

In this lesson we will see how to enter uppercase letters and special characters, and to use **word-wrap** to allow continuous typing. You will type the indicated title and paragraph using Word for Windows. You will save the document, edit it, and then save it again.

Typing the title line

- Hold down the **Shift** key while pressing **s** to capitalize the S in Solving

- Type the rest of the title **Solving Retirement Income Problems** using the Shift key when needed

- Press **Enter** to end the line

- Press **Enter** to leave a blank line before the start of the next paragraph

Typing the paragraph

- Press **Tab** to indent the first line of the paragraph five spaces (0.5 inches). Remember: Word has default settings for tabs (every 5 spaces, ½ inch)

- Type the paragraph as shown below. **<u>DO NOT</u>** press **Enter** until you reach the end of the paragraph. The word-wrap feature of Word will end the lines of the paragraph for you where needed. The **Enter** key is used to end the paragraph and move the cursor down a line and to the left margin.

"It is one of the ironies of retirement planning that the people who are in the best position to save are middle aged-yet the time to start saving is when you're young"(Jacobs 9). What do you see yourself doing when you retire? Taking a cruise to the far corners of the world or a long vacation to visit the grandchildren? Many of us think of retirement as a time in the far-distant future when we will finally have enough time to do what we have always dreamed of. Early retirement planning provides young married couples a financially secure retirement income.

🖐 Press **Enter** after you have typed the last sentence in the paragraph

When you have finished, your paragraph should look similar to the example below:

To Save the document

🖐 Insert a formatted floppy disk into the disk drive

🖐 Point to the **Save** button   in the Tool Bar

🖐 Click the left mouse button

🖐 Click on the **Save in** box arrow

🖐 Point to the **3 ½ Floppy [A:]**

This is what your screen should look like:

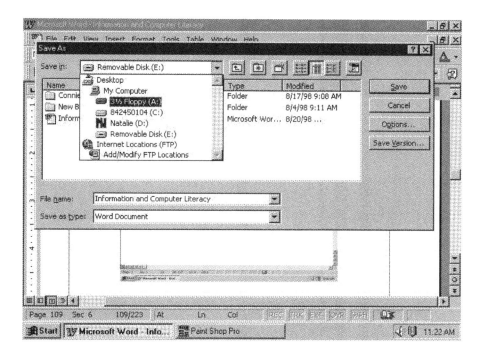

🖰 Click on the selection

🖰 Click on the **File name** box; be sure the window is empty. If it isn't empty use the backspace or delete key to delete the contents.

🖰 With the File name box empty, type the name **TERM1** as the document file name

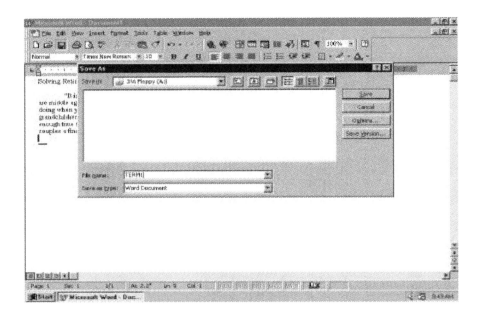

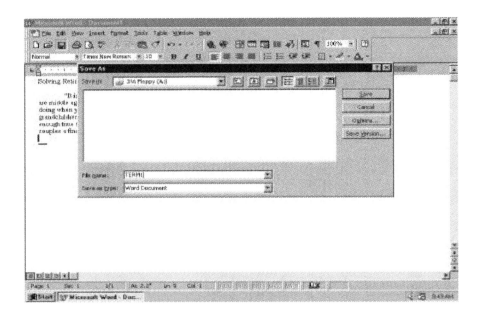 Click on the **Save** button at the right

Word will save the paragraph you have typed on your floppy disk with the name TERM1. Read through the paragraph you've typed and saved.

 Now correct any errors you might have made. Move the cursor to the errors in the document and use the following keys appropriately to make the needed corrections.

If you don't remember the ways to move the cursor around in the document, look at the Cursor Movement definitions at the beginning of this section.

Note to the Student:

If you have pressed the **Insert** key, **OVR** will be displayed in the bottom right corner of your screen, indicating Overstrike mode. When you type in **Overstrike** mode, whatever character you press will overwrite or replace the character above the cursor. Be very careful and selective about using **Overstrike** mode.

If **OVR** is not displayed you are in **Insert** mode. When you are in **Insert** mode, whatever character you press is inserted at the cursor position. The characters to the right of the cursor are pushed one position to the right for every character you type. You can make your corrections and delete any unneeded characters afterwards.

***It is much safer for beginners to type and make corrections in **Insert** mode.

To Resave the document

🖰 Point to the **Save** button   in the Standard toolbar

🖰 Click the left mouse button. Your document will automatically save to your disk under the File name you previously gave it (TERM1).

To Close the document

🖰 Point to **File** in the menu bar

🖰 Click the left mouse button to display the following menu list:

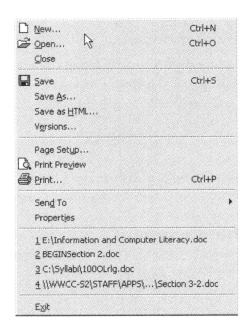

☞ Click on **Close**. You will now have a blank window.

To Exit the Word program

☞ Point to **File** in the menu bar

☞ Click the left mouse button

Your screen will look similar to the previous window displayed when closing a document. This time choose Exit instead of Close.

☞ Choose **Exit**. If you have made changes to the document and have not saved the changes, Word displays a message asking if you want to save the changes.

☞ Choose the **Yes** button to save the changes if needed, the **No** button to ignore the changes, or the **Cancel** button to return to the document without saving.

Note to the Student:

It is a good habit to clear the screen (close the document) before another document is created or another existing (not active) document is edited (changed). Word allows the opening of multiple document windows. This can be confusing for new Word users, so we don't suggest trying it at this time.

Things to Remember

What is the purpose, function or meaning of each of the following terms or functions?

Default setting

Data

Information

TAB

Delete

Backspace

Insert

Overstrike

Application window

Document window

Insertion line

I-beam

Word-wrap

LESSON 8
ON-LINE HELP

In this lesson you are going to open the Word program and look at the Help feature.

🖱 Click on the **Start** icon

🖱 Move the mouse pointer up to **Programs**

🖱 Move the pointer to the right and highlight **Microsoft Office 97**

🖱 Move the pointer to the right and click **Microsoft Word 97**

This is what your screen should look like:

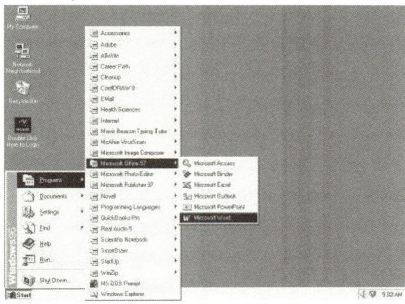

Word 97 has a new help feature called Office Assistant. The Office Assistant is an on-screen, interactive program that provides tips and helps guide you to the right help information quickly.

When you close the Office Assistant window a small Assistant window remains on the screen in case you need to ask for help.

To use the Office Assistant feature:

☞ Click on the **Office Assistant** button **?** on the Standard toolbar, located at the far right of the standard toolbar that looks like this:

After clicking this button, your screen should look like this:

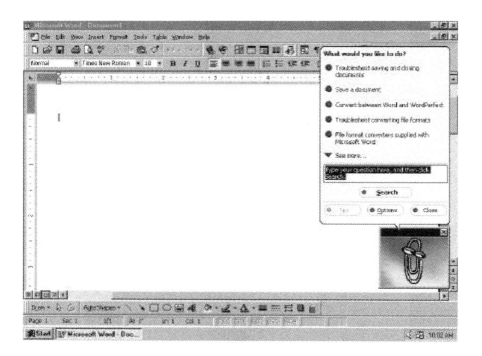

This is what your screen should look like:

🖱 Click on the **Close** button to close the Office Assistant window. The Assistant (paper-clip personality) should remain in the lower right corner of the screen.

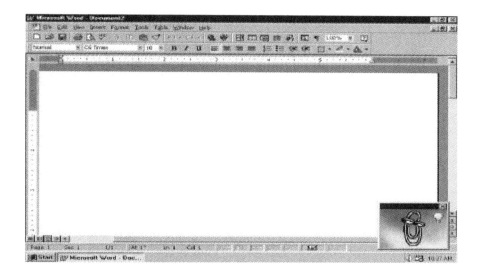

We want to get help on saving a document.

🖱 Move the pointer to the Assistant in the lower right corner of the screen; Click

🖱 Move the pointer to the **Save a document** selection in the Office Assistant window; Click

A window is displayed that explains save options. Read and scroll through the text. At the bottom of the explanation is a list of options. This is what your screen should look like when you reach the bottom of the text explanation:

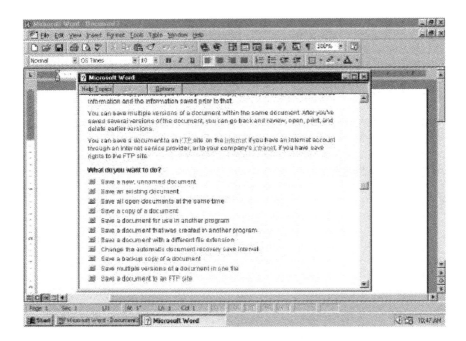

We want detailed help on saving an existing document.

Click **Save and existing document** selection. This is what your screen should look like:

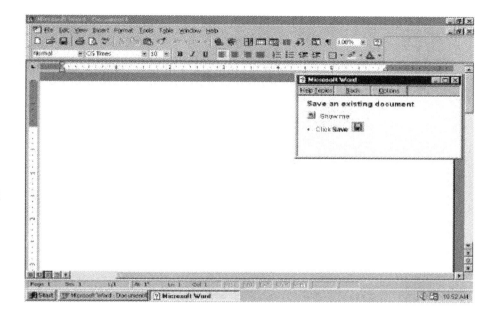

 Click the **Show me** option

The pointer arrow will move to the **Save** button   in the File menu and display an explanation. This is what your screen should look like:

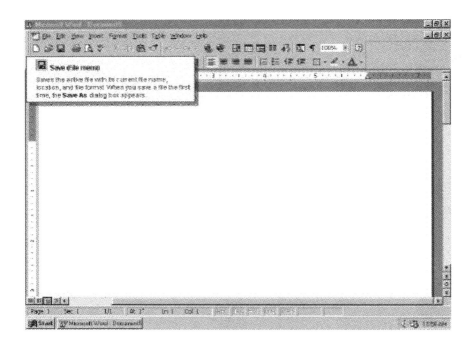

To Close the help window

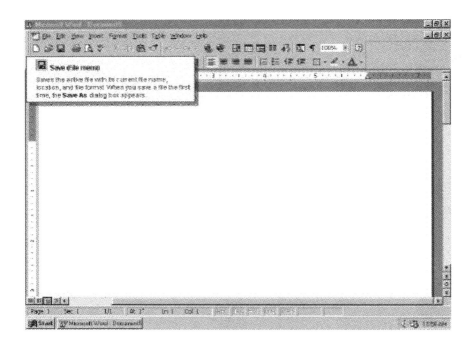 Move the mouse pointer out of the help screen onto the blank document screen and click.

You can also use the Help feature by choosing Help in the Standard Menu bar. Let's look at this option.

Point to **Help** in the Standard Menu bar and click.

This is what your screen should look like:

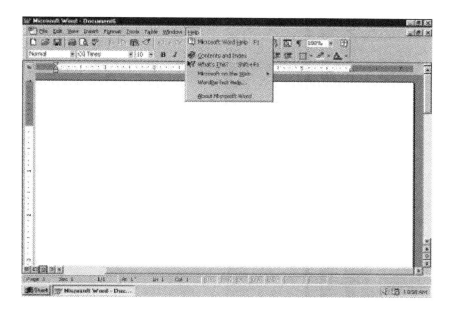

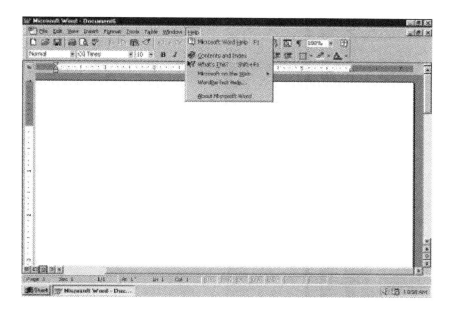 Click on ? **What's This**. The pointer changes to an arrow with a question mark attached. You can point at any selection/button in a toolbar and a help screen will open explaining what it does.

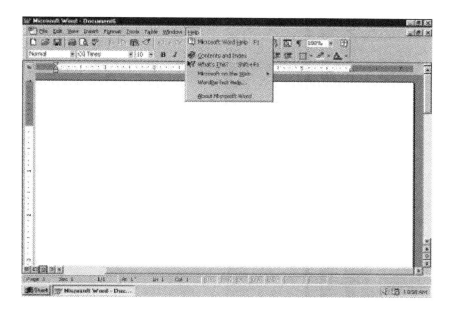 Point at the **Save** button in the Standard toolbar. The same window will open that you saw earlier explaining the Save command.

Use the steps you learned earlier to exit the help window (click on the blank screen).

We are going to look at the Contents and Index option in the Help menu.

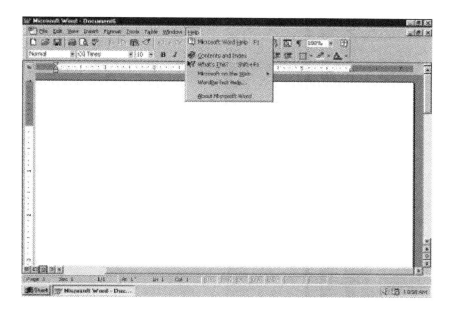 Click **Help** in the Standard Menu bar

 Point to **Contents and Index**; Click

A screen will appear showing two choices:

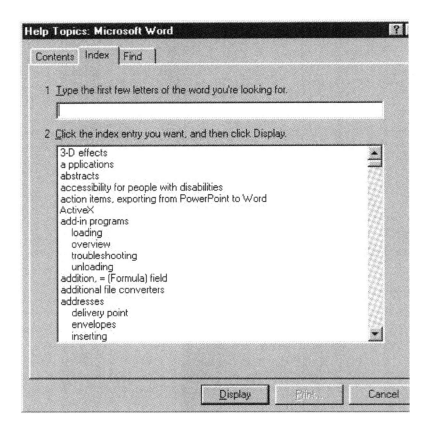

The first choice has you type in the first or first few letters of the topic you want help on.

The second choice alphabetically lists subjects that you can scroll through to look for the topic you are seeking. We are going to use choice number one.

⌐ Type the letter **S** to get information on **saving documents**

A list of options starting with S is displayed as shown in the following figure.

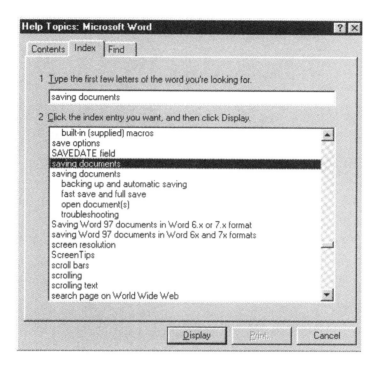

🖑 Click on **saving documents**

🖑 Click on the **Display** button at the bottom of the screen

🖑 Click on the option **"Best place to store documents"**

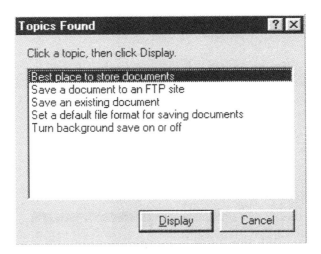

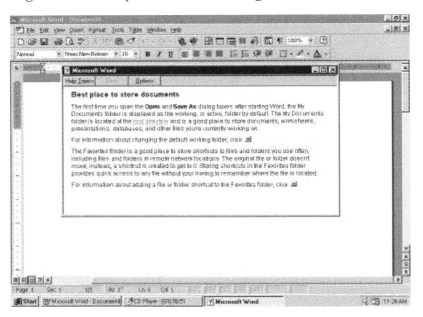

Click on the **Display** button

Read the information given using the scroll arrows at the right to move up and down through the screen.

✍ To **Exit** the Help feature: Click on the **Close** button (**X**) in the top right corner of the window. Word takes you back to the document window where you started.

The best way to learn to use the Help feature is to practice. Try getting help on several buttons in the Toolbars using the Office Assistant. Use the Help option in the Standard menu bar to get help on some different areas in Word, like Open or Indent.

Note to the Student: If you want a printed copy of the Help information you can print by choosing the Options selection after reading the topic information. Click on Print Topics then click on OK.

✍ **Exit** Word

Things to Remember

Office Assistant

Help from the Toolbar

Index

Exit Help

Assignment (do this only if your instructor requests it)

Print a copy of the Help information on each of the following:

❖   Print

❖

❖

❖   Closing a document

❖   Increase indent

LESSON 9
EDITING A DOCUMENT

In this lesson you are going to open Word 97 and retrieve the document you typed and saved in Lesson 7, then insert some text into the document.

Using the steps you learned in the previous lesson:

- Open **Microsoft Word 97**

- Place your 3½ " disk in the disk drive

- Click on the **Open** button in the Standard toolbar

This is what your screen should look like:

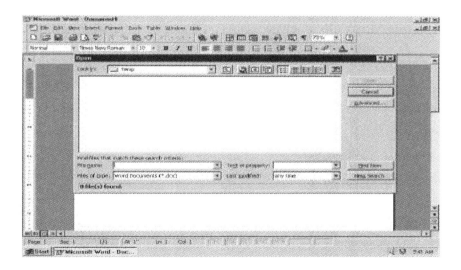

- Click on the **Look in**: box arrow

- Move the pointer to **3½ Floppy [A:]**

This is what your screen should something like the following:

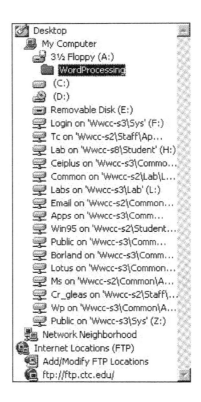

Your computer may not show as many different drives as the above figure. The computer shown is connected to a very large network. It is likely that your computer only shows three or four drive choices.

🖰   Click on **3½ Floppy [A:]**

🖰   Click on **Open**

Displayed in the open window will be the contents of your disk, the TERM1 file

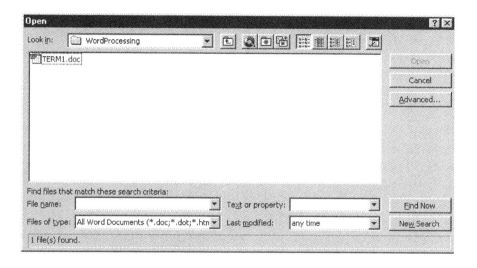

🖱 Click on **TERM1**

🖱 Click on **Open**, at the right

A copy of the TERM1 document will be retrieved from your disk into memory and displayed on the screen for you to work with. The TERM1 document that is now displayed on the screen should look very similar to the following, except there will not be any underlined words on your screen:

Solving Retirement Income Problems

　　"It is one of the ironies of retirement planning that the people who are in the best position to save are middle aged-yet the time to start saving is when you're young"(Jacobs 9). What do you see yourself doing when you retire? Taking a cruise to the far corners of the world or a long vacation to visit the grandchildren? Many of us think of retirement as a time in the far-distant future when we will finally have enough time to do what we have always dreamed of. Early retirement planning provides young married couples a financially secure retirement income.

You are to replace the underlined words with different words. Be sure that you are in **Insert** mode. (Refer to Lesson 6 if you don't remember the difference between Insert and Overstrike modes.)

- Place the cursor (insertion line) on or under the **a** in the first underlined phrase, **a long**.

- Type the words **an extended**.

- Using the Delete key, delete the underlined words **a long**.

- Using the same method, replace the underlined word **time** with the word **period**. Don't forget to delete the original word **time**.

Insert a sentence into the paragraph

- Place the cursor (insertion line) in front of the last sentence in the paragraph starting **Early retirement**.

- Press the spacebar to insert a blank space before the new sentence.

- Type the following sentence:

What ever you hope to do at retirement, it will take retirement income to accomplish what you dream of doing.

- The sentence should be followed by a space.

This is what your document should now look like:

Solving Retirement Income Problems

"It is one of the ironies of retirement planning that the people who
are in the best position to save are middle aged—yet the time to start
saving is when you're young"[Jacobs 9]. What do you see yourself doing
when you retire? Taking a cruise to the far corners of the world or an
extended vacation to visit the grandchildren? Many of us think of
retirement as a period in the far-distant future when we will finally have
enough time to do what we have always dreamed of. What ever you hope
to do at retirement, it will take retirement income to accomplish what
you dream of doing. Early retirement planning provides young married
couples a financially secure retirement income.

Resave your document with the same name

🖰 Point to the **Save** button   in the Standard Toolbar

🖰 Click. This will save your file on your disk with the same
file name (TERM1).

To Close the document and Exit Word

🖰 Point to **File** in the Standard menu

🖰 Click the left mouse button

🖰 Choose **Close**. This will close the TERM1 document.

🖰 Click on **File** in the Standard menu

🖰 Click on **Exit**. This selection will allow you to exit the
Word program.

Things to Remember

What is the purpose, function or meaning of each of the following terms or functions?

Open the document

Insert

Overstrike

LESSON 10
MOVING TEXT BLOCKS

In this lesson you are going to open the TERM1 document, insert additional text, and move blocks of text to new locations in the document.

Using the steps you learned in the previous lesson:

☞ Open the **TERM1** document.

The TERM1 document is now displayed on the screen and should look like this:

Solving Retirement Income Problems

"It is one of the ironies of retirement planning that the people who are in the best position to save are middle aged-yet the time to start saving is when you're young" (Jacobs 9). What do you see yourself doing when you retire? Taking a cruise to the far corners of the world or an extended vacation to visit the grandchildren? Many of us think of retirement as a period in the far-distant future when we will finally have enough time to do what we have always dreamed of. What ever you hope to do at retirement, it will take retirement income to accomplish what you dream of doing. Early retirement planning provides young married couples a financially secure retirement income.

Inserting paragraphs into a document

You will now insert two paragraphs into the beginning of the TERM1 document. Be sure that you are in INSERT mode, refer to Lesson 6 if you don't remember the difference between INSERT and OVERSTRIKE modes. Remember, when in INSERT mode all text that is already on the screen will move to the right of the cursor as you type in new text. (This is what is supposed to happen.)

Review the new document paragraphs that follow. Notice that the phrase **Retirement Planning Strategies** is underlined. There are two methods you can use when underlining a word or group of words. Shown below are two ways of underlining text. You will underline text later in this lesson using one of these methods.

1. Before typing the capital R in Retirement, turn the underline feature on by pointing at the underline button [**U**] in the Formatting toolbar and clicking on it.

OR

2. If you have already typed the text **Retirement Planning Strategies**, block the text (the block designates the section of text that you want to do something to) and then underline it.

🖰 Point to the **R** in Retirement, hold down the left mouse button, and drag the mouse to the right until the phrase **Retirement Planning Strategies** is highlighted. Release the left mouse button. Point to the Underline button [**U**] in the Formatting toolbar and click on it.

Insert new paragraphs

🖰 Place the cursor at the beginning of the line (at the tab) that begins **"It is one of the ironies . . .**

Remember: When you're inserting text in a paragraph, the text to the right of the cursor keeps moving to the right as you type.

🖰 Now type the following paragraphs (using TAB to indent each paragraph, capitalization, punctuation, underlining where necessary, and ending each paragraph by pressing the ENTER key):

New Paragraphs:

      How can young married couples, that are just start-ing out, get started in saving money in today's world of

inflation, high taxes and plastic credit card world? If they could find a small amount of money to save, where and how can they find the right place to invest it for secure returns? There are ways to select and start building a nest egg for retirement and ways to increase the size of that nest egg.

After the marriage ceremony most young couples think about buying a home, starting a family, and paying all the bills that seem to come in a never-ending stream. Retirement could be the last thing on their minds. However, Nick Stinnett, a marriage counselor, states in the book <u>Retirement Planning Strategies</u>, this is an excellent time to lay the foundation for later years. Retirement normally consists of company pensions, personal savings and Social Security. All too often, most of us do not have these options to count on when we retire, so to sit comfortably in the future, it is necessary to plan, save and invest on our own (8).

Your document should look like the following with the new paragraphs inserted:

Solving Retirement Income Problems

|How can young married couples, that are just starting out, get started in saving money in today's world of inflation, high taxes and plastic credit card world? If they could find a small amount of money to save, where and how can they find the right place to invest it for secure returns? There are ways to select and start building a nest egg for retirement and ways to increase the size of that nest egg.

After the marriage ceremony most young couples think about buying a home, starting a family, and paying all the bills that seem to come in a never-ending stream. Retirement could be the last thing on their minds. However, Nick Stinnett, a marriage counselor, states in the book Retirement Planning Strategies, this is an excellent time to lay the foundation for later years. Retirement normally consists of company pensions, personal savings, and Social Security. All too often, most of us do not have these options to count on when we retire, so to sit comfortably in the future, it is necessary to plan, save and invest on our own (8).

"It is one of the ironies of retirement planning that the people who

After pressing Enter to end the second inserted paragraph, be sure the original paragraph starting "It is one of the ironies" is indented with a Tab. If it isn't indented insert a Tab using the skills you've learned.

If your document has an extra Tab at the beginning of the last paragraph ("It is one of the ironies), delete it. The paragraph should only be indented one Tab.

Resave your document with the same name.

⌐ Save your document using the steps you learned in previous lessons.

Moving Text

Now you are going to move the last paragraph that starts **"It is one of the ironies** to the beginning of the document, making it the first paragraph.

🖱 Place the cursor at the beginning of the line (at the left margin) that begins **"It is one of the ironies**

🖱 While holding down the left mouse button, drag the pointer down the text until the whole paragraph is highlighted, release the mouse button.

🖱 Point to the **Cut** button   on the Standard toolbar, Click

After the paragraph has been Cut it disappears from the screen. It has been placed in memory on a clipboard, waiting for your use.

🖱 Position the cursor at the beginning of the line (at the left margin) that starts **How can young married**

🖱 Point to the **Paste** button on the Standard toolbar; Click

The paragraph that starts **"It is one of the ironies** is now the first paragraph of the document. This is what your document should look like after successfully moving the paragraph:

Solving Retirement Income Problems

"It is one of the ironies of retirement planning that the people who are in the best position to save are middle aged—yet the time to start saving is when you're young"(Jacobs 9). What do you see yourself doing when you retire? Taking a cruise to the far corners of the world or an extended vacation to visit the grandchildren? Many of us think of retirement as a period in the far-distant future when we will finally have enough time to do what we have always dreamed of. What ever you hope to do at retirement, it will take retirement income to accomplish what you dream of doing. Early retirement planning provides young married couples a financially secure retirement income.

How can young married couples, that are just starting out, get started in saving money in today's world of inflation, high taxes and plastic credit card world? If they could find a small amount of money to save, where and how can they find the right place to invest it for secure returns? There are ways to select and start building a nest egg for retirement and ways to increase the size of that nest egg.

After the marriage ceremony most young couples think about

Save and Exit

🖰 Resave the document with the same name (TERM1), using the steps you have learned throughout your lessons.

🖰 Exit Word using previously learned steps

Note to the Student:

When you move or copy a block of text, like a paragraph, the computer removes the indicated text from the screen and puts it on a clipboard (temporary storage out of sight) until you indicate where you want it placed back into your document and paste it.

Things to Remember

What is the purpose, function or meaning of each of the following terms?

Open the Document

Insertion line (cursor)

TAB

Cut

Paste

Clipboard

Underline

LESSON 11
FORMATTING THE TEXT

In this lesson you are going to open the TERM1 document, center a line of text, indent the quotation (a paragraph), and change the line spacing in the document.

🖰 Open the TERM1 document using steps you've learned.

The TERM1 document should now be displayed on your screen.

Centering Text

To center the title (the title is considered a paragraph, it ends with an Enter):

🖰 Move the cursor (insertion line) to the **S** in Solving

🖰 Point to the Centered Text icon in the Formatting toolbar; Click

If you don't know which icon is used to center text here are some helpful hints:

❖ Slowly move the pointer to each icon and read the description that is shown to find the icon that centers text..

❖ Use the Help feature to look up centering text.

❖ Look at the description of the toolbars given at the beginning of the Word processing section of the text.

This is what the centered title should look like:

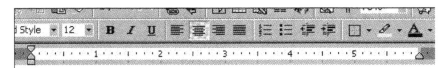

> Solving Retirement Income Problems
>
> "It is one of the ironies of retirement planning that the people who are in the best position to save are middle aged—yet the time to start saving is when you're young"[Jacobs 9]. What do you see yourself doing when you retire? Taking a cruise to the far corners of the world or an extended vacation to visit the grandchildren? Many of us think of

Indent Text

Now you are going to indent the quote in the first paragraph. An indent moves the text (a paragraph) in five spaces like a TAB, but it also creates a temporary left margin. The indent is active until the end of a paragraph.

We want only the quote to be indented, so we need to make it a separate paragraph.

- Place the cursor on the **W** (What) that starts the second sentence of the paragraph.

- Press the **Enter** key to separate the quote from the rest of the paragraph.

- Place the cursor at the beginning of the line (at the left margin) that starts **"It is one of the ironies . . .**

- Point to the **Increase Indent** icon on the right side of the Formatting toolbar (see figure) and Click

🖰 Press the **Backspace** key. This will delete the TAB that was used to begin the paragraph. The cursor should now be under the quotation mark(").

If the paragraph starting **What do you see** is indented:

🖰 Place the cursor on the **W** in **What** and press the **Backspace** key to delete the Tab.

Now only the quote in the first paragraph is indented and the paragraph looks like this:

Solving Retirement Income Problems

"It is one of the ironies of retirement planning that the people who are in the best position to save are middle aged—yet the time to start saving is when you're young"(Jacobs 9).

What do you see yourself doing when you retire? Taking a cruise to the far corners of the world or an extended vacation to visit the grandchildren? Many of us think of retirement as a period in the far-|

Changing the Line Spacing

When changing the line spacing of a document you need to understand that you are changing the format (the way a document looks) not the actual content. You must select the text you want to work with in the document to change the line spacing for that text. You can also change the line spacing of a single paragraph by choosing Paragraph from Format in the Menu bar.

🖰 Move the cursor to the top of the document using either the Up Arrow key or the PgUp key.

If the document is several pages, you can hold down the Ctrl key and press the Home key (Ctrl+Home) then type a 1 to indicate page 1 of the document. Enter, then click on Close. This will place the cursor in the top left corner of the document.

🖱 While holding down the left mouse button, drag the pointer down the text until all paragraphs are highlighted

🖱 Select **Format** from the Menu bar

🖱 Point to the **Paragraph** command; Click

🖱 Point to the **Line Spacing** box arrow   ; Click

🖱 Point to **Double** (indicating double spacing) Click to choose it

🖱 Click on the **OK** button, Word will return you to the document

** Short cut method:

After you have highlighted all the paragraphs:

🖱 Hold down the **Ctrl** key and the number **2** together. This sets the line spacing at double for all highlighted text. Ctrl+2 also works for a paragraph.

The document is now double-spaced. The following example shows only part of the document, but gives you an idea of how your document should look:

> Solving Retirement Income Problems
>
> "It is one of the ironies of retirement planning that the people who are in the best position to save are middle aged—yet the time to start saving is when you're young"(Jacobs 9).
>
> What do you see yourself doing when you retire? Taking a cruise to the far corners of the world or an extended vacation to visit the grandchildren? Many of us think of retirement as a period in the far

If your document is not double-spaced, go to the top of the document and repeat the steps.

🖰 Resave your document to your disk with the same name, TERM1.

Things to Remember

What is the purpose, function, or meaning of each of the following terms or functions?

Delete

Center

Indent

Format

Line spacing

LESSON 12
PRINTING THE DOCUMENT

In this lesson you will print the TERM1 document that you have typed and edited. Word for Windows makes printing a document pretty easy.

Print Setup

Let us look at the print window to make sure that everything is set up the way we need. **YOU ARE NOT GOING TO PRINT AT THIS TIME!**

🖑 Point to **File** in the Menu bar; Click

🖑 Highlight **Print**; Click

The Print window will be displayed on the screen and look similar to this:

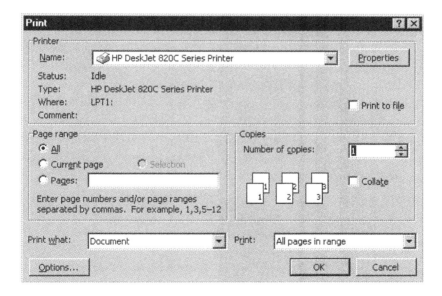

Here is an explanation of the items in the window:

Option	Action
Printer	The selected printer is displayed
Page range	• All - will print all pages in the document
	• Current Page - will print the page where the cursor is currently located
	• Pages - this allows you to print a selected range of pages. If you ha a twenty page document and you only wanted to print the first 5 pages you would click on Pages, type 1-5 in the box and only the indicated pages would be printed.
Number of copies	The default value is set at 1 copy. Since you want to print only one cop of the document, this setting does not need to be changed.
Print what	Document - this indicates the document currently on the screen or activ in the form that is needed.
Print	All Pages in Range - this is the default setting and what is usually needed

If you are in a computer lab that is networked, you may need to select a printer. Check with your instructor about the print-er selected.

To Select a Printer

With the Print window open,

🖱 Click on the Printer box arrow

A list of available printers is displayed.

🖱 Highlight the printer you want to use (if you don't know which printers are available for your use, ask your instructor or the lab Monitor for assistance).

🖱 Click on your selection to choose it

DO NOT PRINT AT THIS TIME!

Normally, when you are ready to print you would click OK, but bear with us for a little longer.

⌐ Click on **Cancel** since you don't want to print at this time.

Printing the Document

⌐ Open the TERM1 document using the steps you have learned. If you don't remember how, look at a previous lesson to review the steps.

Now your TERM1 document is active and displayed on the screen.

You want to print 1 copy of all the pages in the document.

Since you have checked the Print window and selected the correct printer you should be ready to print. If any adjustments need to be made, do so when you open the Print window.

⌐ Click on **File** in the Menu bar

⌐ Click on **Print**

Check the selections in the Print window.

⌐ Click on **OK** to print a copy of the TERM1 document.

Your instructor may request that you turn in this copy of the TERM1 document.

⌐ Close your document and Exit Word using the steps you have learned.

Note to the student: Once you have set the Print window up the way you want it, resave your file. In the future you can print from the Print icon in the Standard toolbar.

Things to Remember

Answer the following questions to review the print feature.

1. How do you indicate that you want to print all the pages in the document?

2. How do you print one page of a multiple page document?

3. How do you print more than one copy of a document?

4. How do you select a new or different printer to use?

5. When would you use the Print icon in the Standard toolbar to print your document?

LESSON 13
THE WINDOWS EXPLORER

In this lesson, you will learn to manage and organize the files on your disk using the functions of the Windows Explorer.

Specifically, you will learn how:

❖ to name a file;

❖ to create a folder and why;

❖ to copy or move a file from one folder to another; and

❖ to delete a file.

Disk Storage Organization and Folders

If you are given the task of organizing an office's correspondence files, you would perhaps designate different drawers of a file cabinet for each different major category or topic. Next you might break each drawer into different subjects and then arrange each subject area by the author/receiver of the letter. This type of organization allows you to find any particular document by its subject and recipient later. All you need to remember is the general organization plan of the files. When finished, your file cabinet may have a structure like that shown in Figure 1:

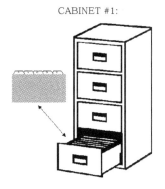

CABINET #1:

DRAWER #1 - SALES

    FILE #1 - RUBBER BANDS

    TAB #1 - CONNIE

    TAB #2 - JOE

  FILE #2 - PAPER CLIPS
    TAB #1 - RON

DRAWER #2 - PURCHASES

    FILE #1 - ...

Figure 1. File Cabinet and Its Organization.

To help someone find a letter written to Connie about the sales of rubber bands, you could draw them a map. Better yet, provide them with a path of the names to follow:

Cabinet #1, Drawer #1, File #1, Tab #1.

What if you were able to organize the files of your programs, data and documents of the computer in the same way? That is, organize these files so that all of the files that belong together are placed separately from each of the other groups of files. Windows 95 has a disk management facility that allows you to organize your disks in this manner. But, instead of cabinets, drawers, files and tabs, these divisions are called *folders*. Folders are logical divisions of your hard disk or diskette that can be used to group together files of the same type or subject. To accomplish this you create a separate folder for each category, type or subject of document. This creates a predicable path by which you can find the files later just like in the file cabinet above.

You can create a folder anytime the need for a new folder occurs. The folder could be for a class, like ENGLISH, or a program, like WINWORD. The folder might be for a person, JESSICA, or a project, PAPER, or interest area, SOCCER. Folders can be for anything and can be named just about anything, as long as you use a legal Windows filename.

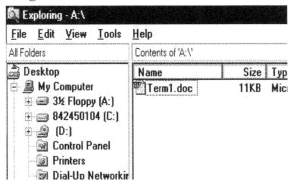

Figure 2. The Windows Explorer showing the A: Drive

When you format your disk, all existing files and folders are removed. After formatting, your disk is blank and contains only one folder. This folder is called the root folder. The symbol \ (backslash) is used to represent the root folder. The root folder is like the whole of the file cabinet in the example above. The root folder is the beginning, base, or overall folder of the disk. It is called the root folder because all other folders branch from this root.

Our file cabinet can best illustrate folders. Each drawer of the file cabinet is like a "super folder." If we create a folder for each of the drawers in our file cabinet example, it may look something like that shown in Figure 3. Notice how the folders "Rubber Bands" and "Paper Clips" have folders in them for Connie, Joe, and Ron. Folders can contain files or other folders. These "sub-folders" can also contain folders.

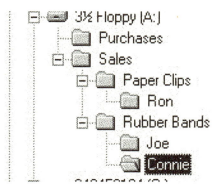

Figure 3. The File Cabinet Converted to Windows 95 Folders

Each of the drawers, files and tabs of the cabinet are now separate folders. When converted into Windows 95 folders, the path to the Connie's folder would be stated as A:, Sales, Rubber Bands, Connie.

Within the file cabinet, each drawer, folder, and file breaks the subject matter into smaller and more specific groupings. Each of these smaller sub-topic groupings creates a folder, or a folder within a folder. Any folder may contain folders, along with programs and document files, and these folders can themselves contain folders. For example, we could create a sub-folder within the sub-folder JOE for each month. Folders may be created at any level. Remember that the disk does not come pre-formatted with folder groupings. You create your own folder groupings. Folders are for your convenience. Use care and common sense in naming the folders and they will provide you with an easily remembered and logical path to your data files and programs.

Creating a Folder and a File

In the following exercise, you will create a folder on your diskette, create a Notepad file and save it to the new folder, rename the file, delete the file, and delete the folder from your diskette.

☜ If you are not already there, take the necessary actions to display the Windows Desktop.

Place your formatted diskette in the appropriate drive.

☜ Click the Start Button located on the Taskbar. This will display the Start Menu as shown in Figure 4.

Figure 4. The Windows 95 Start Menu

🖰 Click on the Programs option to display the Program Menu. It should look something like the one in Figure 5.

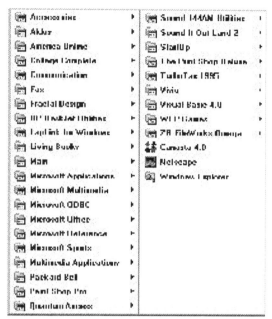

Figure 5. A Sample Windows 95 Program Menu

🖰 On the Program Menu, find the shortcut entry for the Windows Explorer, shown in Figure 6.

Figure 6. The Windows Explorer Shortcut on the Program Menu

🖰 Click on the Windows Explorer shortcut. The Windows Explorer application should fill the desktop and look similar to Figure 7.

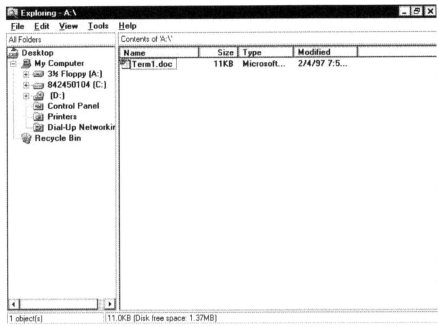

Figure 7. The Windows Explorer Display

The Windows Explorer display is divided into two frames. The left frame displays the storage devices attached to the computer and the primary folders of Windows 95. In can also display the folders contained on each storage device. The right frame is used to display the folders and files within a particular folder.

🖑   In the left frame, find the A: disk drive icon and click on it. The A: entry should be highlighted now. The TERM1 file that your created in previous lessons should appear in the right frame.

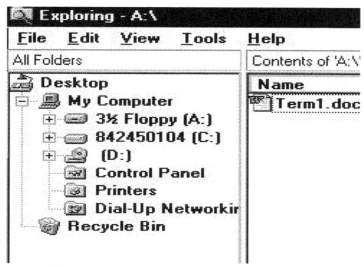

Figure 8. The Windows Explorer Left Panel

🖱 Now find the word "File" on the menu bar and click on it. This should display the File Menu. The first choice on this menu is "New... ", click on the New... option. It should display the pull-down menu shown in Figure 9.

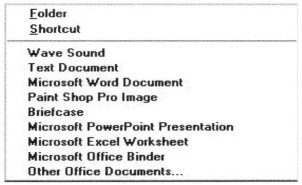

Figure 9. The File New... Option Menu

🖰 Click on the "Folder" choice. This will add a new folder to the right frame with the name "New Folder." The name should be highlighted for you to enter a name for the folder, as shown in Figure 10.

Contents of 'A:\'			
Name	**Size**	**Type**	**Modified**
📄 Term1.doc	11KB	Microsoft...	2/4/97 7:5...
📁 New Folder		File Folder	2/4/97 8:3...

y [A:]
]4 (C:]

Figure 10. New Folder Added to the A: drive

🖰 With the folder name highlighted, enter a new name for the folder. Use your first and last name. Press the Enter key when you've finished.

🖰 Double-click the A: icon. The newly created and renamed folder should appear as a sub-element of the A: drive as illustrated in Figure 11.

🖰 Repeat the steps you've just used to add one additional new folder to the A: drive. Name this folder "Documents". When you've completed this step your display should look like the one shown in Figure 11.

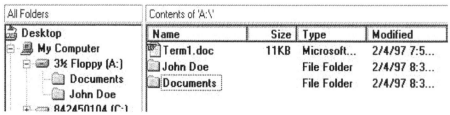

Figure 11. The A: Drive Structure After Adding Documents Folder

🖑 Using the right mouse button, click on the folder that has your name. A shortcut menu, like the one shown in Figure 56 should appear. Choose from this menu the choice "Rename."

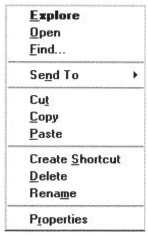

Figure 12. The Windows Explorer Shortcut Menu

🖑 Rename the folder "Spreadsheets" and press the enter key or click the left mouse button anywhere in the Explorer right panel outside of the folder name box.

The display in the right panel of your Windows Explorer display should look like that shown in Figure 13.

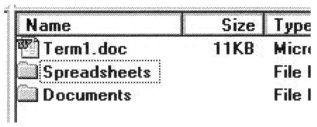

Figure 13. Folders After Changes.

✌ Click on the Document Folder icon and select the File
New menu options to add a new "Microsoft Word
Document". This choice should be on the list provided by
the New menu item, as shown in Figure 14.

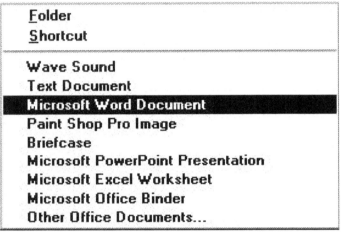

Folder

Shortcut

Wave Sound

Text Document

Microsoft Word Document

Paint Shop Pro Image

Briefcase

Microsoft PowerPoint Presentation

Microsoft Excel Worksheet

Microsoft Office Binder

Other Office Documents...

Figure 14. New Option Menu

A new item should be shown in the right frame of the Windows
Explorer display representing a new document named "New
Microsoft Word Document.doc", shown as the "Before" image
in Figure 15. With the document name highlighted, use the
shortcut menu to rename this document "How I Spent My
Summer.doc". Be sure to add the period and "doc" at the end of
the filename. This tells Windows 95 what kind of file it is.

Contents of 'A:\Documents'

Name	Size	Type
New Microsoft Word Docum...	5KB	Micros

Before Rename

After Rename

Figure 15. Text Document File Before and After Rename Action

The above steps do not represent the most efficient way to create a document file. This exercise was included to allow you to see how long file names for documents and folders are used. But, since we are here, let's open a file from the Windows Explorer, change it, and save it.

🖑 Double-click the document icon associated with the file "How I Spent My Summer.doc". The file and the Microsoft Word application should open and be ready for your next action as shown in Figure 16.

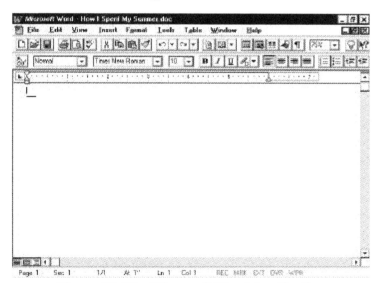

Figure 16. The Microsoft Word Application.

🖱 The cursor is ready in the upper left corner of the Word document window. Enter a few lines on what you did, or wished you'd done, last summer. (Don't worry about spelling or punctuation!)

Figure 17. Toolbar Print Button

🖱 When you've finished entering your story, choose the Save option from the File menu. If you'd like to print your document, do so by choosing Print from the File menu or by clicking on the printer button found on the toolbar (shown in Figure 17).

🖱 Close the Microsoft Word application by clicking on the Close button in the right corner of the window. This will return you to the Windows Explorer.

🖱 Highlight your "How I Spent My Summer" document by clicking on it.

🖱 Click on either the File menu choice or the shortcut menu and choose "Delete." If this choice is not shown, repeat the previous step to insure that the file is chosen (highlighted).

🖱 This removes the document from your disk.

🖱 Click on the disk drive symbol labeled as "3½ Floppy (A:)" in the left frame. This will return you to the root folder of the diskette.

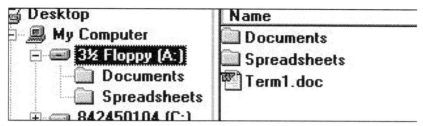

Figure 17. Windows Explorer Display After Returning to A: Drive Root.

🖑 Click on the "TERM1.DOC" document in the right frame and while holding down the mouse button, point to the "Documents" folder in the left frame and release the mouse button. This action will move the "TERM1.DOC" document into the "Documents" folder. Click on the "Documents" folder to verify that the document was moved. The document should appear in the right frame display for the "Documents" folder.

This action is called "Drag and Drop" because you "grab" the file, drag it into place and drop it where you want it. This same action can be accomplished by highlighting the file and using the "Move" or "Cut" and "Paste" functions on either the File menu or the Toolbar.

🖑 Close the Windows Explorer to return to the Desktop.

Things to Remember

Answer or perform the activities of the following questions and exercises.

1. Why would you create folders on your disk?

2. What feature of Windows 95 is used to find, move or manage folders and files?

3. Create a new folder in the root folder your disk. Add a new Microsoft Word document to the new folder using only:

   a. The Toolbar and Menu choices and options

   b. Shortcut menus.

4. Using drag and drop, move the file created in #3 above from one folder to another and then delete the file using the shortcut menu.

Terms

Define and explain each of the following terms. Remember that Lesson 4 talks about files and filenames if you need to review.

drag & drop

file

filename

folder

path

root folder

shortcut menu

short filename

LESSON 14
MANAGING FILES

In this lesson you will continue to work with your files and folders.

⌐ Start Microsoft Word

In the last lesson you created two folders (DOCUMENT and SPREADSHEETS) on your diskette and moved your TERM1.DOC into the DOCUMENT directory.

The location of your files becomes important when you open files from now on. If you follow the steps you have used in the past to open your file you'll notice that the file doesn't appear when you click on your diskette drive in the Drive window. Remember that you moved your file from the root directory (folder) into the DOCUMENT folder. You can't see or open the TERM1.DOC file until you open the DOUCMENT folder.

Let's open your TERM1.DOC file.

⌐ Point to the **Open** icon   ; Click

⌐ Point to the **Look In** arrow box   ; Click

⌐ Select **3 ½ " A**: or the drive holding your diskette; Click

Your screen should look like this:

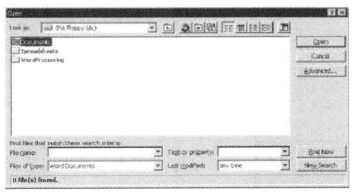

🖰 Click on the DOCUMENT folder you created. Remember; this is where you have stored your TERM1.DOC file.

🖰 Click on **Open**

🖰 Point to the TERM1.DOC; Click

🖰 Click on **Open**

Your TERM1 file will be active in memory and displayed on the screen.

🖰 Close the TERM1.DOC file and Exit Word

Things to Remember

1. When you have moved files into a folder, what must you do before you can open your file?

2. What folders did you create on your diskette?

3. The folders you created on your diskette are in what directory?

LESSON 15
COMBINING DOCUMENTS

In this lesson you are going to open the TERM1.DOC file that you printed in Lesson 10 and add an existing file to the end of it. This will create the new version of the research paper on which you have been working. If you read through this paper you will notice that it isn't complete. Part of the pages were deleted to cut down on the length; printing the full document took too long and caused the death of too many trees.

🖰 Open Word for Windows

🖰 Open the TERM1.DOC file on your diskette, using the steps you learned in the previous lesson. (Remember that TERM1.DOC is located in the DOCUMENT folder.)

The TERM1.DOC file will be displayed on the screen.

🖰 Move the cursor to the bottom of the TERM1 document

Your screen should look like this:

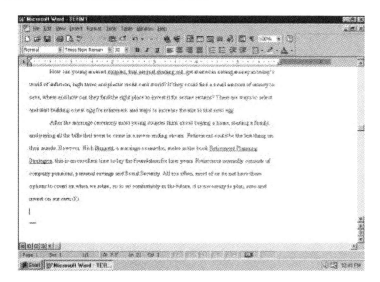

🖱 If the cursor is behind the (8) you need to be at the left margin on the next line, so press the END key then press ENTER.

Next you will insert a file containing the second half of the research paper, TERM2.DOC, at the end of the TERM1 document. The TERM2.DOC file is provided for this course either on a student disk or the file could be stored on the school network drive for student use.

Check with your instructor for the location of the TERM2.DOC file. If the TERM2.DOC is stored on a student disk follow these steps:

🖱 Remove your disk from the floppy disk drive and insert the Student disk

🖱 Click on **Insert** in the Menu bar

🖱 Click on **File**

🖱 Click on the 3 ½ " disk in the "Look in:" box arrow if it is not currently selected

🖱 Open the WORD folder on the Student disk

🖱 Click on the TERM2.DOC file, then OK

If the TERM2.DOC file is stored on a network drive (an example of file location is used) follow these steps using the location your instructor indicated:

🖱 Click on **Insert** in the Menu bar

🖱 Click on **File**

🖱 Click on the **"Look in:"** box arrow

🖱 Move the pointer down to highlight the network drive indicated

🖱 We are using **"Common on 'Wwcc-s2\Lab\Labs'…** , click on it

🖱 Point to the **CT100** folder; Click

🖱 Click on **Open**

🖱 Point to the **Bookdisk** folder; Click

🖱 Click on **Open**

🖱 Point to WORD folder; Click

🖱 Click on **Open**

🖱 Click on the TERM2.DOC file

🖱 Click on **OK**

The TERM2 document is now added to the bottom of TERM1.

🖱 Insert your disk into the disk drive

Now you will save this document with the new name of FULL-TERM. By saving the file with a new name you retain your TERM1 document in case you need it later on.

🖱 Click on **File** in the Menu bar

🖱 Click on **Save As**

🖱 In the File name box type **FULLTERM**

Your screen should look like this:

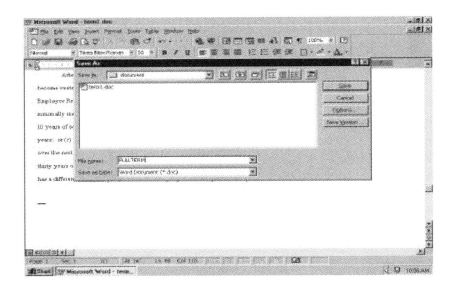

✍ Click on **Save**

Through the previous steps we have combined two documents into one. The Insert/File method used above is only one way this can be accomplished.

READ the following. *DO NOT perform the steps indicated.*

Another way of combining files:

❖ Open the TERM1.DOC file from your disk

❖ Open a second file indicated on the screen as DOCU-MENT 2 (this file would be the TERM2.DOC)

❖ Choose Select All from Edit in the Menu bar

❖ Cut the selected text; close Document 2

❖ Paste TERM2 (the cut selected text) at the bottom of the TERM1 file

❖ To keep the two original files intact you would save the combined files with a new name.

🖰 Close the FULLTERM document using the steps you've learned.

🖰 Exit Word

Things to Remember

1. What is one way of combining two files and creating a new file?

2. Of the two methods talked about in this lesson, which do you think would be the easiest to do?

SECTION 3

ELECTRONIC SPREADSHEETS

Occasionally you need to use numbers in your document. The logical way to view numbers is in columns and rows, or sometimes called tables. There are several ways to add these columns and rows of numbers into a word processor document. In this section we will learn how to use a spreadsheet or a table to manipulate numbers and to show graphically the relationship between the values through charts and graphs.

To this point in your lessons, you have used Microsoft Windows 95 and Microsoft Word 97. Microsoft Word 97 is great for typing text into a document. It can do many things very well, as you have learned. The Microsoft Office suite has other software that is better for working with numbers. One of the other software programs is Microsoft Excel 97, a spreadsheet package.

Microsoft Excel 97 allows you to organize primarily--numeric data in many different ways and forms. It allows you to easily make calculations. You may want to make "what if" decisions, by quickly changing a value or multiple values to see what happens under varying or changing situations. It allows you to create charts or graphs to show the relationship between the values graphically. Microsoft Excel 97 will let you sort or query (ask questions) of the data to see what is the largest/smallest, or for example, see how many items are more than $100.00.

In this section you will use the Microsoft Excel 97 to create a workbook, to develop a retirement budget, and a pie chart of the budget using an Microsoft Excel 97 worksheet and chart.

Microsoft Excel 97 has three major components:

Workbooks and worksheets: Worksheets allow the user to enter data, calculate the data, and to format the data. Workbooks, like any book, are made up of sheets. In this case workbooks are made up of individual worksheets. Worksheets in the workbook can be made to link data together. For example monthly worksheets can be cumulated into a yearly summary on one worksheet.

Charts: Charts are graphic representations of the data in the worksheet(s) or the workbook. There are many different types and variations of charts. These charts can be for example, line, bar, pie, or even scatter charts. They can be two or three dimensional, scaled, and even customized to adapt to the users' needs. Microsoft Excel 97 contains user friendly tools called Wizards, to help the user to create charts.

Database: The Database component of Microsoft Excel 97 allows the user to sort, query, search, for specific data contained in the worksheet.

LESSON 16
STRUCTURE & COMPONENTS

In this lesson you will identify the basic parts of a Microsoft Excel 97 workbook and worksheets

The figure below is an example of a worksheet.

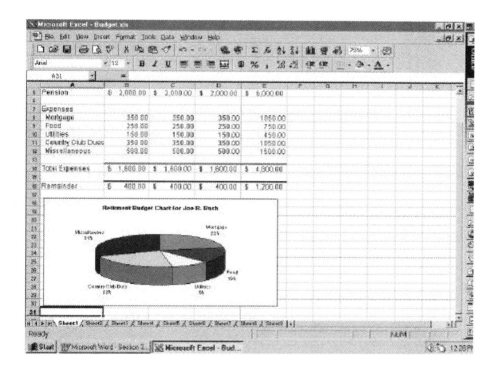

To Start Microsoft Excel 97

First of all, Microsoft Windows 95 must be running on your computer.

There are several ways that Microsoft Excel 97 can be started:

❖   The Start Button

❖   Short cut Icon on desk top

❖   Microsoft Office tool bar

You instructor, or lab assistant, will show you the best way for you to start Microsoft Excel 97 on your computer system. Both the desktop and the set up of Microsoft Windows may vary from computer system to computer system.

When Microsoft Excel 97 is running you will see a workbook with a blank worksheet like the example shown below:

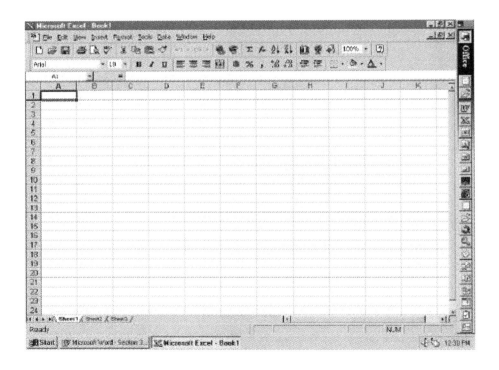

Parts of a Microsoft Excel 97 Workbook

Workbook
A **workbook** is made up initially of 16 blank worksheets. You may add or delete worksheets as needed, or add charts as separate sheets as well.

Worksheet
Each **worksheet** is made up of columns and rows.

Columns
Columns are indicated by a letter(s) at the top of each column.

Rows
Rows are indicated by a number(s) at the beginning of the row at the left of the worksheet.

Cells
Cells are created at the intersection of each column and row. The intersecting column letter and row number identifies a cell. For example at the intersection of column B and row 3 would be cell B3. Therefore B3 is known as the **cell address** for the cell at the intersection of column B and row 3. Cells are the units that hold numbers, labels, comments, etc. (or, in other words, all the data that can be on a worksheet).

Current Cell
The Current Cell is cell shown by the heavy border. More important, the current cell is also the active cell - the place that receives the action or data as you work. As you enter data, or tell Microsoft Excel 97 to do something, it will do it to the current cell or active cell. When you type data into the active cell and enter it, that data will be placed into the cell indicated by

the cell pointer. We will work on how to type and enter data into cells later.

Mouse Pointer

To use the mouse pointing device with Microsoft Excel 97, find the mouse pointer. The mouse pointer is usually a **big block arrow**, a **big block cross**, a **bold plus sign**, or a **bold plus sign with arrow heads horizontally**. Moving the mouse controls the mouse pointer. Its purpose is to position the cell pointer, to complete some action or command by clicking, or to call up the Microsoft Excel 97 menu.

Workbook Window

The workbook window includes the area of the current worksheet that can be seen. There are 256 columns and 16,384 rows on each worksheet, so most of the current worksheet can not be seen until you scroll or move the cell pointer to areas off the screen. Each workbook is made up of 16 worksheet tabs at the bottom of the screen. Remember that you can add worksheets and charts as needed. You can move between worksheets by clicking on a worksheet tab to see a different worksheet.

Scroll Arrows, Scroll Bars and Tab Scrolling Buttons

The scroll arrows, scroll bars, and tab scrolling buttons control the movement on the worksheet, and allows view of parts of the worksheet that is not in the current worksheet's window. They allow you to see cells outside what is currently on the monitor's screen.

Worksheet Tabs

The worksheet tabs show the different worksheets and charts as separate items and allow you to click on each to move or make them active.

Title, Menu, Formula Bars & Tool Bars

The Title bar shows the title of the current active worksheet. The Menu bar contains the titles of Microsoft Excel 97's pull down menus. The Standard toolbar has icon buttons allowing specific tasks and actions to be completed. The Formatting toolbar specifically allows you to format or change how the text on the spreadsheet looks or is formatted. The Formula bar is the area directly above the worksheet columns showing the current active cell's address or location, the current cell's contents, and some small button icon to help when entering data.

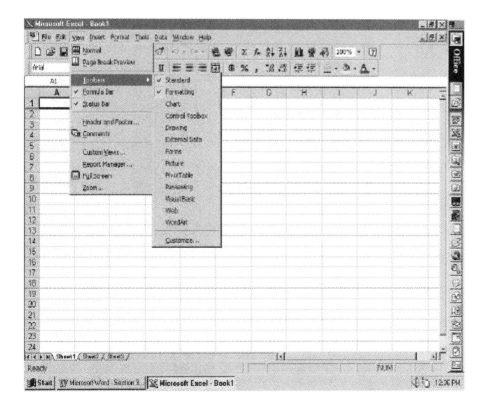

Above is an example of a workbook window with 2 major tool bars showing. Each of these toolbars is very important and will be used extensively to complete the following lessons. As you can see, there are several tool bars available. Usually the Standard and Formatting Toolbars are showing. If they are not showing, or others are showing you can go to the Main menu and choose View, then choose Toolbars and click the check marks on or off to include the tool bars you wish to see.

The following figure identifies the parts of the workbook window:

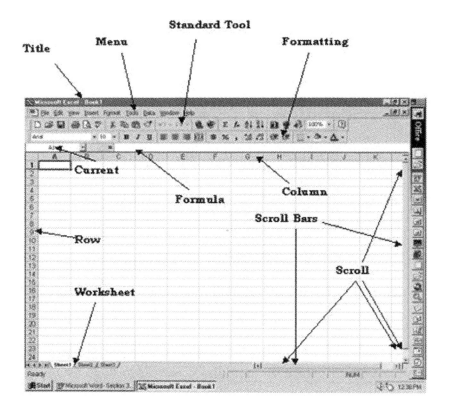

Tool Bars and Menus

Title Bar

Double click on the Microsoft Excel 97 icon to close Microsoft Excel 97, or click to see menu choices for the Microsoft Excel 97 program.

The Main Menu

The Standard Tool Bar

The Formatting Tool Bar

The Formula Bar

Things to Remember

Terms

Workbook	Mouse Pointer	Workbook Window
Worksheet	Scroll Arrows	Scroll Bars
Column	Tab Scrolling Buttons	Title Bar
Row	Menu Bar	Formula Bar
Cell	Standard Toolbar	Formatting Toolbar
Cell Pointer	Current Cell	

LESSON 17
ENTERING & DELETING DATA

The many concepts introduced in this lesson will be needed in later lessons. Do not try to learn in detail all of these concepts now. What you need to know will be shown and referred to again.

In this lesson you will learn:

❖ The icons of the Excel 97 tool bars

❖ How to enter data

❖ How to correct and/or delete data

❖ Moving on the worksheet

❖ The difference between labels and values

❖ How to Exit the program

Excel Toolbars

In the next few pages we will show the Microsoft Excel 97 toolbars and give descriptions of the buttons, menus, and choices on them. Each tool bar has a name, and has items grouped together which do similar types of things.

☞ To complete this lesson you must have Microsoft Excel 97 running and a worksheet visible on your screen.

The Menu Bar's name indicates what its main purpose is. The Menu Bar contains the Microsoft Excel 97 main menu items

The Workbook Menu Bar

☞ To display the contents of one of the menu items, point the mouse pointer at the menu and click.

This is an example of what the screen could look like if you were to choose Edit on the Main Menu:

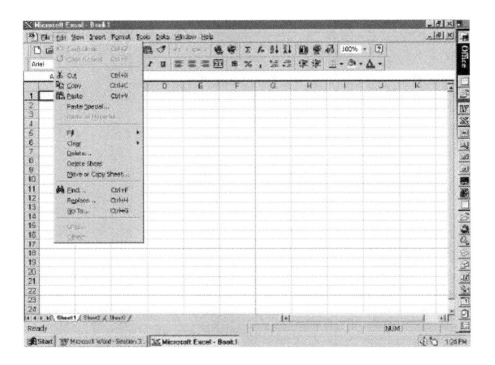

Each menu choice may be activated by:

1. Clicking the mouse pointer on the item on the menu bar

Once any menu item is active you may arrow to another item on the menu bar by using left or right arrows, or by clicking on the sub-item in the menu.

Or by,

2. Holding down the ALT + the first letter of the menu item

The Formatting Toolbar

The Formatting Toolbar has icons for formatting the data on the worksheets

Information regarding each icon can be found through the help menu or by pointing the mouse at the icon and waiting for Microsoft Excel 97 to display the name of the icon.

The Standard Toolbar

The Standard Toolbar shows short cuts that can be done on the Menu or Formula Bar.

The Standard Toolbar is similar to the Formatting Toolbar because information regarding each icon can be found either through the help menu or by pointing the mouse at the icon and waiting for Microsoft Excel 97 to display the name of the icon.

The Formula Toolbar

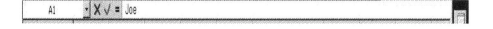

The Formula Toolbar's primary function is to show the active cell address and the actual contents of the current active cell. The Formula Toolbar also allows editing of text or formulas in the current active cell. Some buttons in the Formula Toolbar

only show when data is being entered into the cell. These buttons are identified below.

 The GoTo icon. Click on this icon and enter the cell location you wish to go to.

 The Cancel icon. Click on this icon to cancel the typing or entry in this cell.

 The Enter icon. Click on this icon to enter the typing or entry in this cell.

 The Function Wizard icon. Click on this icon to start the Functions Wizard.

Starting Microsoft Excel 97

Starting Microsoft Excel 97 is similar to starting Microsoft Word 97 or any other Microsoft Windows 95 application program. If you need specific help with starting an application program in Microsoft Windows 95, please see your instructor for specific help.

🖱 Start Excel

🖱 Make sure cell A1 is the current active cell. If it is not the current active move the cell pointer in cell A1. See below.

Moving the cell pointer

The following are methods of moving the cell pointer.

Arrow keys   use the arrow keys to move the cell
                            pointer to the desired cell

Mouse   click on the desired cell

Home Key   moves the cell pointer to the left edge of
                            the worksheet

Ctrl+Home key   the Ctrl+Home key is located up and to
                            the right of the enter key, it will move the
                            cell pointer to cell A1

Page Up   moves the cell pointer one computer
                            screen width up

Page Down   moves the cell pointer one computer
                            screen width down

 or F5 Key   moves the cell pointer to the cell address
                            you type in

End Key   used to take the cell pointer to the end of
                            either a filled or empty row or column of
                            consecutive cells. The end key is used in
                            conjunction with an arrow key, i.e.: End
                            and arrow key right

Note: the formula bar shows cell A1 as the current active cell,
and the word Joe is being type into the current active cell, (cell
A1).

Entering data into a cell

1. Move to the cell that you want the data to be entered, and type.

2. Use the enter key to enter the data once it is type into the formula bar.

❖ Or Clicking on the [✓] to enter the data

❖ Or Use an arrow key to move to an adjacent cell, this automatically enters the data as you move the cell pointer

❖ Or Click on the [✕] to cancel the data you have typed so far

🖱 Enter your name into the cell.

Your name will show in the cell, as in the example worksheet showing Joe's name typed and entered into cell A1.

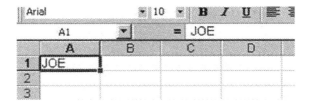

Making typing corrections

Sometimes as we type, we may make an error on the keyboard. I am sure most of you have excellent keyboarding skills, but I know that I make frequent goofs that need fixing.

There are two different times when typing corrections can be made:

1. We can see errors as we are typing and the data has not been entered yet.

Corrections:

Backspace Key   The backspace key erases the
                             characters as the cursor backs up

X icon on formula bar   Click the Cancel typing icon to erase
                             all the characters.

2. When the data has been entered into the cell.

Corrections:

Typeover   Retyping, or typeover the old data to enter
                             the new or corrected information

F2   In Microsoft Excel 97 the special function
                             key F2 is used to edit a cell's data. By
                             pressing the F2 key the data is shown in
                             the cell and can be edited one character at
                             a time by using the arrow keys, left and
                             right to locate the cursor, then using the
                             delete or backspace keys to complete the
                             editing. Enter to complete the editing

Formula Bar   You may also edit the contents of the
                             active cell by making corrections directly
                             within the data shown in the formula bar

Delete Key   When pressed this key will remove the
                             data in the current active cell, while the
                             Mode Indicator says Ready. If the Mode
                             Indicator says Edit, the delete key will
                             delete only one character at a time

Delete data

Sometimes we may need to remove, or delete, data from a cell after it has been entered. Now we will remove your name from cell A1.

☞ Move the cell pointer back to cell A1 if it is not the current active cell.

There are several ways to delete data from the current active cell after the data has been entered.

1. Striking the delete key.

2. Using the Edit menu by clicking on Edit in the Menu Bar then Delete, or using the Alt+E keys together, then D for Delete. Notice if you use this method Microsoft Excel 97 will prompt you how to shift the cells. This important to know because the whole column or row will shift, but not the whole worksheet. You may want to go try this.

3. Using the short cut menu method, click the right mouse button. Make Active the cell that contains the data to be deleted. Click on the right mouse button and choose delete. Note the same caution as mentioned before that the software will shift the cells.

The following example shows the short cut menu being used and the delete choice activated.

The next picture shows the prompt from Microsoft Excel 97 to shift the cells after you delete the current active cell.

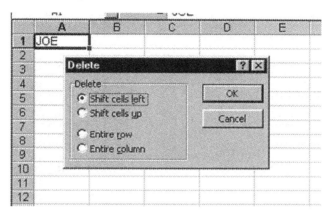

Note: You can shift the cells up, down, left, or right.

🖱 Using what you have learned, delete your name from cell A1.

Exiting Microsoft Excel 97

🖱 Choose File in the main menu bar at the top of the work-sheet.

🖱 Choose Exit in the file menu bar at the top of the work-sheet as shown in the following graphic.

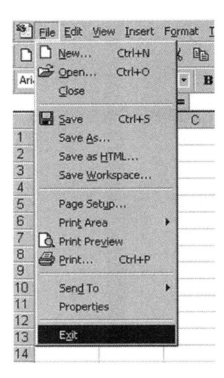

A dialog box will pop-up telling you the worksheet has not been saved. Since this worksheet was created as a practice exercise, do not save it.

Choose No

At this point we do not want to save this workbook.

Note: You can use a shortcut method by clicking on the Microsoft Excel 97 icon above the main menu bar to close the worksheet, but more about that later.

Things to Remember

Terms

Actual Wizard

Align

Align Across Column

Alt + a letter

Arrow Keys

Auto Sum

Backspace

Bold

Borders

Cancel Typing

Chart Wizard

Clear

Color

Copy

Cut

Delete

Delete Key

Drawing

Edit

End

Enter

Enter

F2

F5

Font

Format

Format Painter

Formatting Toolbar

Formula Bar

Function Wizard

Go To

Help

Home

Italic

Mode indicator

New Workbook

Open

Page Down

Page Up

Paste

Print

Print Preview

Repeat

Save

Sort

Spelling

Standard Toolbar

Text Box

Tip Wizard

Typeover

Underline

Undo

Zoom

LESSON 18
CREATING A WORKSHEET

Now let's make a budget for your retirement using what we know. The worksheet you will create in this section will be merged into a Microsoft Word 97 document in a later lesson.

In this lesson you will:

❖ Create a worksheet that contains row and column labels

❖ Save the worksheet

🖑 Start the Microsoft Excel 97 program and have a blank worksheet displayed

Entering Data

Labels and Values

Before we start entering data let's define one more term, Data. All data entered in to Microsoft Excel 97 is received in only two forms. Data is entered either as a label or as a value. Labels are usually used as titles or descriptions. Values usually are numbers used for calculations in some type of mathematical action.

A value can include only the following characters:

❖ All numbers, i.e. 1234567890

❖ The characters,(for doing the math),   + - (@ # $

❖ Function names are considered numeric, i.e. =SUM(E3:E8)

❖ We will learn more about this later.

Labels must begin with at least one of the following characters:

❖ Alphabetical characters, i.e. A,B,C,D, e, f, g, h, i, etc.

❖ Special characters: ' " ^ ~ ! % & _ \ | >

Let's enter the labels for our budget. Enter labels shown below in the cells indicated. Use the arrow keys or a mouse to move to each new cell and enter the data typed.

Remember, you have learned how to enter and correct data in the previous lesson.

To create a worksheet title, follow the instructions below:

🖰 Move to cell B1.

🖰 Type: Retirement Budget for Joe R. Bush. Be sure to replace the words "Joe R. Bush" with your own name as you type.

Note: As you type look at the character showing in the current active cell and also in the Formula Bar

🖰 Then hit the Enter key to enter what you have typed.

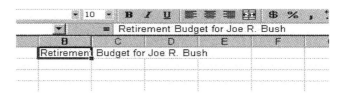

Your worksheet should look like the above example, except your name should be substituted for Joe's.

If you are having problems entering the data, or if for some reason it is not typed correctly, refer back to the previous lesson for help on entering and typing corrections.

Now that we have a worksheet title, we need to put in some row and column titles.

🖰 Move the cell pointer to cell A5

🖱 Type and enter the word **Pension**

🖱 Move cell pointer to cell A7

🖱 Type and enter the word **Expenses**

🖱 Type and enter the labels for cells A8 through A12 using the following information

🖱 Type in **2 spaces** at the beginning of these labels to indent them:

Cell	Label
A8	Mortgage
A9	Food
A10	Utilities
A11	Country Club Dues
A12	Miscellaneous
B3	Jan

This is what your screen should look like:

	A	B	C	D	E
1		Retirement Budget for Joe R. Bush			
2					
3		Jan			
4					
5	Pension				
6					
7	Expenses				
8	Mortgage				
9	Food				
10	Utilities				
11	Country Club Dues				
12	Miscellaneous				
13					
14	Total Expenses				
15					
16	Remainder				
17					
18					
19					

Copying labels

Now we need to get the remaining labels in for Feb. and Mar in cells C3 and D3. But, rather than typing them in, we will learn how easy it is to copy data.

🖰 Make cell B3 the current active cell by clicking on it.

🖰 Copy the label Jan to cell C3 and D3.

Instructions to copy:

🖰 Put the mouse pointer on the bottom right corner of the cell, on the small box. When your pointer is on the box the pointer will turn into a **bold narrow cross**.

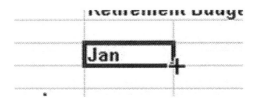

🖰 With the pointer in this mode press and hold the left mouse button and drag to the next 2 cells. To drag is to move with the mouse button down. Drop the contents into the next 2 cells to the by letting the mouse button up. This is basically how we copy the contents cell to adjacent cells.

This is what your screen should look like:

Notice that when we copy the word Jan. to adjacent cells the word Jan. changes to Feb. and Mar., the program is copying logical sequence of months. It will copy other logical sequences as well as other numbers, and/or labels

🖰 Move cell pointer to cell E3

🖰 Type and enter the word 1st Qtr.

🖰 Move cell pointer to cell E4

🖰 Type and enter the word Total

When you have completed these steps your worksheet should look like the example below.

A	B	C	D	E	F
	Retirement Budget for Joe R. Bush				
	Jan	Feb	Mar	1st Qtr	
				Total	
Pension					

Saving the worksheet

Saving the workbook allows you to put a copy of your work on a disk for safe keeping, and for later work.

🖰 Click on File in the Menu Bar.

🖰 Choose Save As

The Save As command displays a dialog box that allows you to name and place the file in the location you wish.

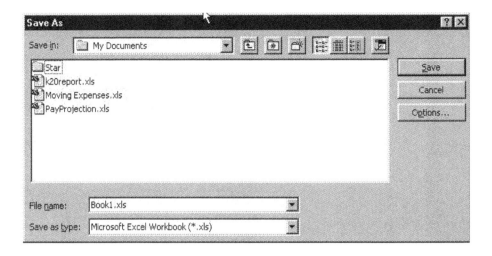

🖰 In the "Save In:" box, choose 31/2" Floppy drive (A:), or use the arrow to make the A: drive current.

🖰 Click on the folder named Spreadsheets, you created this folder earlier in the text.

🖰 In the "File Name" box type **budget**

Your screen should look like the example below.

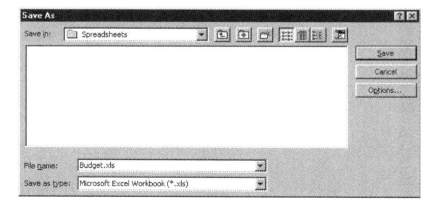

🖰 Click on the Save button

Remember that you may use up to 32 characters for a file name with Microsoft Windows 95 software, if your machine is configured for long file names. Also, Microsoft Windows 95 does not use extensions as older versions of software do. You may want to ask your instructor regarding both of these features.

Things to Remember

Terms
Help:

    Search Button

    Show Topics

Working Directory

Tools Menu:

    Options

    General Tab

Label

Value

File Save As

    Default File Location

LESSON 19
ENTERING VALUES

Now that you have created and saved the worksheet we named Budget, we can continue developing that worksheet. We will now learn some additional concepts in this lesson.

In this lesson you will learn how to:

❖ Enter Values

❖ Copy Values

❖ Re-save the Worksheet

Now we will retrieve the file Budget from the last lesson that you saved on your disk.

🖰 With your disk in the floppy disk drive, Start the Microsoft Excel 97.

🖰 Choose Open from the menu

🖰 Choose the 3 ½ "floppy disk drive

🖰 Choose the Spreadsheets folder and click Open

🖰 Choose Budget and click Open to load the file

The screen should look like this after you retrieve your worksheet:

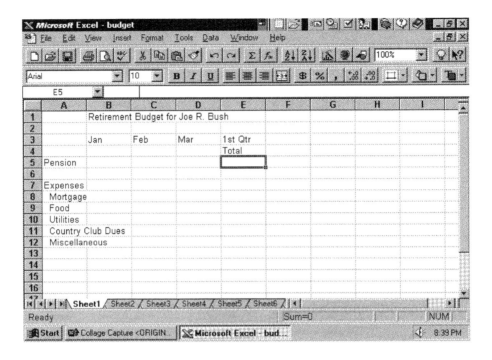

Entering Values and Labels

Please follow the instructions below. If you make a mistake while you are typing, remember the typing correction methods from the previous lessons.

🖰 Enter the values listed below into the cells indicated.

Cell	Value
B5	2000
B8	350
B9	250
B10	150
B11	350

B12   500

The screen should look like this after entering the values:

	A	B	C	D	E
1		Retirement Budget for Joe R. Bush			
2					
3		Jan	Feb	Mar	1st Qtr
4					Total
5	Pension	2000			
6					
7	Expenses				
8	Mortgage	350			
9	Food	250			
10	Utilities	150			
11	Country C	350			
12	Miscellan	500			
13					
14	Total Expenses				
15					
16	Remainder				
17					

🖰 In cell A14 type the label Total Expenses

🖰 In cell A16 type the label Remainder

The screen should now look like the above example.

Copying Values

Now copy the all values in the Jan column to the Feb and Mar columns. You will use skills learned in the previous lesson on copying the contents of cells.

🖱 Make cell B5 the current active cell by moving to or clicking cell B5. Then, with the mouse pointer on B5 (the mouse pointer as a big block cross) hold down the left mouse button and drag the mouse down to cover all the values.

The screen should look like this:

	A	B	C	
1		**Retirement Budget for J**		
2				
3		**Jan**	**Feb**	**Mar**
4				
5	**Pension**	**2000**		
6				
7	**Expenses**			
8	**Mortgage**	**350**		
9	**Food**	**250**		
10	**Utilities**	**150**		
11	**Country C**	**350**		
12	**Miscellan**	**500**		
13				
14	**Total Expenses**			
15				

🖱 Now put the mouse pointer on the bottom right corner of the darkened area until the mouse point is a small bold cross. Holding down the left mouse button, drag the contents into the next 2 columns and drop the contents by letting go of the mouse button to complete the copy.

The screen should look like this:

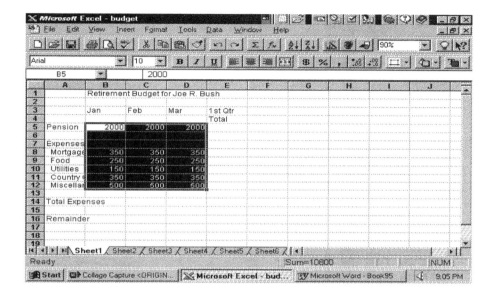

Resaving the Worksheet

Resaving is slightly different than saving the worksheet initially. We could resave the worksheet the same way we did before,
but there is an easier way now that the worksheet has once
been saved.

🖰 From the Menu Bar choose File

🖰 Choose Save

OR

🖰 Click on the ⊞ icon in the Standard Toolbar to save the
file.

Note to the Student:

At times you may wish to edit a document or worksheet and
resave it without disturbing or changing the original. If this is

the case, you must change the file name. If so, we would use the Save As option as we did the first time we saved the document or worksheet.

🖰 Now you can exit Microsoft Excel 97 without losing your updated worksheet, because your changes have been saved to your disk.

Things to Remember

Terms

File:

New

Open

Close

Save

Save As

Entering Values

Entering Labels

Copy

Delete

A typing Corrections Exercise for you to try!

On the student disk are some Microsoft Excel 97 files to help you understand how to correct typing mistakes, copy, move, and delete data on a worksheet. Complete the exercises listed below. They will help you better understand how to work with Microsoft Excel 97.

To start the exercise make sure that Microsoft Excel 97 is running on your computer and a workbook is up and on the screen.

🖰 In the Spreadsheets folder, open the file named "TYPOS.XLS"

☞ The file contains the instructions to complete the exercise.

LESSON 20
FORMULAS & FUNCTIONS

In this lesson, you will retrieve the BUDGET.XLS worksheet file and add totals for the 3 months for each item using formulas and functions.

❖ Use Worksheet calculations by creating formulas and functions built into Microsoft Excel 97.

❖ Copy formulas and functions.

❖ Underline and Bold text.

🖰 Start the Microsoft Excel 97 program and load the BUDGET.XLS file loaded on your computer. Use the steps you have learned from previous lessons. It should look like the example below:

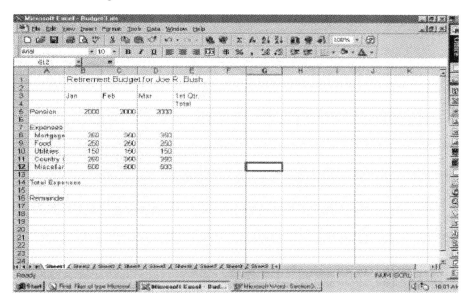

At this point we need to add 3 different calculated amounts.

1. Calculate Total Expenses

2. Calculate the Remainder

3. Calculate the 1st Qtr. Total for each category for the quarter.

Worksheet Calculations

Note: Functions, such as the Sum function, are procedures or formulas built into Microsoft Excel 97. They allow us to build and complete tasks more quickly and efficiently.

To calculate Total Expenses for each month with the Sum function:

🖰 Move the cell pointer to cell B14.

🖰 Click on the ⬚Σ⬚ button, the Auto Sum button.

	A	B	C	D	E
1		Retirement Budget for Joe R. Bush			
2					
3		Jan	Feb	Mar	1st Qtr
4					Total
5	Pension	2000			
6					
7	Expenses				
8	Mortgage	350	350	350	
9	Food	250	250	250	
10	Utilities	150	150	150	
11	Country C	350	350	350	
12	Miscellan	500	500	500	
13					
14	Total Expe	=SUM(B8:B13)			
15					
16	Remainder				
17					

As you can see Microsoft Excel 97 is making a suggestion or wanting to sum the cells B8 through B13. The worksheet should look like the above example.

🖰 Press the enter key to accept the suggested function's parameters =SUM(B8:B13), the range or group of cells B8:B13, suggested by Microsoft Excel 97. Microsoft Excel 97 makes its best guess of what you want to be summed together.

If Microsoft Excel 97 does not make the correct suggestion, =SUM(B8:B13), you may highlight the correct cells. You may show Microsoft Excel 97, B8:B13, by clicking on B8 to make it active and then by holding the cell pointer on the cell, as a large block cross, on B8 and holding down the left mouse button then drag down, highlighting through B13. Enter will complete the process, and the 1600 should show in cell B13, as in the example below:

	A	B	C	D	E	F
1		Retirement Budget for Joe R. Bush				
2						
3		Jan	Feb	Mar	1st Qtr	
4					Total	
5	Pension	2000				
6						
7	Expenses					
8	Mortgage	350	350	350		
9	Food	250	250	250		
10	Utilities	150	150	150		
11	Country C	350	350	350		
12	Miscellan	500	500	500		
13						
14	Total Expe	1600				
15						

An alternative method to the Auto Sum is to manually type in the Sum function. To do this move to cell B14 and type in the following: =SUM(, then move the cell pointer to the top value, dragging and highlighting to the bottom value. The program will build or write in the cell locations for you. You must close the parentheses creating the sum function, =SUM(B8:B13). Enter to finish.

Or,

You may type =SUM (then type the cells B8:B13 and close the parentheses).

You need to know how to type in functions manually, because sometimes the cells you wish to work with will not be adjacent to each other.

To create a function with cells that are not adjacent, you can type them completely manually like the previous example, or you can use the point and click method. To use the point and click method first type =SUM(then holding down the Ctrl key continuously, click on each cell that is to be included in the function's procedure. Close the parentheses creating the function. Enter to accept.

Note to the student:

As you become more familiar with how spreadsheets work you will find that using the suggestions from the program or using the mouse and the Ctrl key to create and build functions in non-adjacent cells is really the easiest ways to complete the task.

🖰 Move the cell pointer to cell C14 and total Feb's values.

🖰 Then complete the total for D14.

Your worksheet should look like the following example:

	A	B	C	D	E	F
1		Retirement Budget for Joe R. Bush				
2						
3		Jan	Feb	Mar	1st Qtr	
4					Total	
5	Pension	2000				
6						
7	Expenses					
8	Mortgage	350	350	350		
9	Food	250	250	250		
10	Utilities	150	150	150		
11	Country C	350	350	350		
12	Miscellan	500	500	500		
13						
14	Total Expe	1600	1600	1600		
15						
16	Remainder					

Other Microsoft Excel 97 Functions:

There are many functions built into Microsoft Excel 97. The =SUM function will be one that you use many times to add values as you build worksheets. Some of the other functions you may use are:

=AVG() To calculate the average of values in a range of cells.

=COUNT() To count the number of values in a range of cells.

=MIN() To calculate the smallest value in a range of cells.

=MAX () To calculate the largest value in a range of cells.

Each set of parenthesis after the function name will contain the cells, or the parameters to be used with the functions, i.e. =SUM(B8:B13).

You will work with these functions in an exercise at the end of this chapter.

Formulas

The Remainder is the difference between the pension, as income, and the Total Expenses. If you were writing this out as a math problem you would write, 2000 - 1600. In a spreadsheet you do not usually use numbers in a formula, you use the cell locations of the numbers. The reason for using the cell address in formulas is to allow us to do "What If" analysis with the worksheet. "What Ifs" are when we want to change a value to see what will happen if this change is made. The calculations on the worksheet will automatically re-calculate. By setting formulas up this way Microsoft Excel 97 is not dealing with the literal current values, but with whatever value is in the cell(s). So the 2000 - 1600 would, and should be, written =B5-B14 with the answer 400 in cell B16. Since we want the entry to be a function or a formula, (do math) the entry must start with an equal sign.

The formula will read   **=B5-B14**.

To calculate the Remainder

- Move the cell pointer to cell B16.

- Type an equal sign =

Note to the student:

When creating formulas, the location of the formula, the cell containing the equal sign (=), is where the answer will show.

- Press the up arrow key to move the cell pointer to the pension income for the first month, cell B5, or click on cell B5.

- Type a minus (-) sign to indicate subtraction.

There are two minus signs on you key board. One on the top right corner of the 10 key pad, and one just right of the 0 at the end of the numbers on the keyboard.

✒ Press the up arrow to move to the total expenses for the first month, cell B14.

The formula should read =B5-B14 in the Formula Bar.

✒ Press **Enter** to complete the formula and enter this into the worksheet.

✒ Use the same process to complete formulas in cells C16 and D16, to complete the Remainder line on the worksheet.

The worksheet should look like the example below.

	A	B	C	D	E
1		Retirement Budget for Joe R. Bush			
2					
3		Jan	Feb	Mar	1st Qtr
4					Total
5	Pension	2000	2000	2000	
6					
7	Expenses				
8	Mortgage	350	350	350	
9	Food	250	250	250	
10	Utilities	150	150	150	
11	Country C	350	350	350	
12	Miscellan	500	500	500	
13					
14	Total Expe	1600	1600	1600	
15					
16	Remainder	400	400	400	
17					
18					

Note to the student:

Often other math operations are needed in formulas. The math functions Microsoft Excel 97 uses are shown below.

ADD	+
SUBTRACT	-
MULTIPLY	*
DIVIDE	/
EXPONETS	^
CONTROL the ORDER of OPERATION	( )

To calculate the 1st Qtr. Total for each category using the Autosum function.

⌐ Move to cell E5.

⌐ Click on the [Σ] Autosum button. It should choose the range B5:D5.

⌐ Enter to complete the function.

You may also use one of the alternative methods discussed earlier in the section.

The worksheet should look like the following example:

	A	B	C	D	E	
E5			=	=SUM(B5:D5)		
1		Retirement Budget for Joe R. Bush				
2						
3		Jan	Feb	Mar	1st Qtr	
4					Total	
5	Pension	2000	2000	2000	6000	
6						
7	Expenses					
8	Mortgage	350	350	350		
9	Food	250	250	250		
10	Utilities	150	150	150		
11	Country C	350	350	350		
12	Miscellani	500	500	500		
13						

Copying formulas

🖱 Move to cell E5 and make it the current active cell.

🖱 Go Edit on the main menu, or click the right mouse button to bring up the Short Cut Menu.

🖱 Choose Copy from the menu.

🖱 Hold down the Ctrl key. (Keep holding it down through the next steps.)

🖱 With Ctrl key down move to cell E8.

🖱 With the Ctrl key still down drag with the Big Block Cross down through to cell E12.

🖱 With the Ctrl key still down, click on cell E14.

🖱 With the Ctrl key still down, click on cell E16. Release the Ctrl key.

🖱 Enter to complete the copy.

🖱 Save the worksheet

🖱 Your worksheet should look like the example below:

	A	B	C	D	E
1		Retirement Budget for Joe R. Bush			
2					
3		Jan	Feb	Mar	1st Qtr
4					Total
5	Pension	2000	2000	2000	6000
6					
7	Expenses				
8	Mortgage	350	350	350	1050
9	Food	250	250	250	750
10	Utilities	150	150	150	450
11	Country C	350	350	350	1050
12	Miscellan	500	500	500	1500
13					
14	Total Expe	1600	1600	1600	4800
15					
16	Remainder	400	400	400	1200
17					

Note to the student:

We can copy data or formulas from one location to another by using several methods. The Short Cut Menu will show options to Edit the worksheet. The Short Cut menu is shown below. To complete the tasks in either the Short Cut menu or the Main menu using the Edit menu the cell or a range of cells must be active or highlighted before the procedure.

The Shortcut menu shown above contains other options for editing the worksheet.

The Clipboard

When data is copied or cut it is held on the Clipboard. The Clipboard is a memory area that holds information while it is being copied or moved from one place to another. The data being copied may be copied or moved from one place on a worksheet to another place on that worksheet, to another worksheet, or other program, such as a word processing document. A copy of the data on the Clipboard stays until new data is copied to the Clipboard.

With a little practice you will be an expert in no time. You will be trying some techniques in the practice exercises at the end of this lesson.

Relative Cell References in formulas

Another fact about copying formulas and functions is that when a formula or function is copied, the cell references are changed to reflect the new location.

Example:

If a formula in cell B3 reads =B1+B2 and is copied to cell C3 the formula will automatically change to reflect the new location by adding 1 to the column letter, and it will read =C1+C2. If the formula is copied down 1 will be added to the row number. For example if a formula in cell C3 is =C1+C2 and is copied down one row then it would read =C2+C3. The term for this automatic formula change when copying is called Relative.

Things to Remember

Terms

 Autosum button

Functions in Microsoft Excel 97

=AVG()	To calculate the average of values in a range of cells.
=COUNT()	To count the number of values in a range of cells.
=MIN()	To calculate the smallest value in a range of cells.
=MAX()	To calculate the largest value in a range of cells.

Formulas

Math Functions

ADD	+
SUBTRACT	-
MULTIPLY	*
DIVIDE	/
EXPONETS	^
CONTORL the ORDER of OPERATION	( )

Working with data (cells) in non-adjacent areas

Ctrl and click

Ctrl and drag

Copying Formulas

     Relative

     Absolute

A Formula and Functions Exercise for you to try!

Using the instructions given in the previous lessons, retrieve the FORMULA.XLS and FUNCTIONS.XLS files from EXCEL folder on the student data disk. Complete the exercises in the order listed; they will help you better understand how to work with Microsoft Excel 97.

Each file contains the instructions to complete the exercise.

LESSON 21
FORMATTING & PRINTING

Now that you've created your budget worksheet, in this lesson you will:

* ❖ Adjust column widths

* ❖ Change the format of specific cells

* ❖ Justify labels

* ❖ Print the worksheet for review.

* ❖ Add lines and borders

🖰 Retrieve the **BUDGET** file, it should look like this:

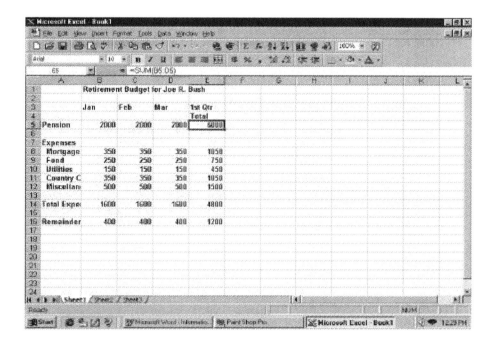

Inserting lines:

✒ Move the cell pointer in cell A13

✒ Highlight the cells A13 through E13 by dragging from A13 to E13. Hold the Ctrl key down and click on cell A15 and drag through cell E15

This is what the screen should look like:

	A	B	C	D	E
1		Retirement Budget for Joe R. Bush			
2					
3		Jan	Feb	Mar	1st Qtr
4					Total
5	Pension	2000	2000	2000	6000
6					
7	Expenses				
8	Mortgage	350	350	350	1050
9	Food	250	250	250	750
10	Utilities	150	150	150	450
11	Country C	350	350	350	1050
12	Miscellan	500	500	500	1500
13					
14	Total Expe	1600	1600	1600	4800
15					
16	Remainder	400	400	400	1200
17					

✒ Click on the Borders button (see following figure) to pull the Border menu down and select the underline option.

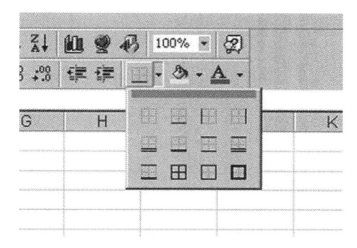

The worksheet should look like the example below.

	A	B	C	D	E
1		Retirement Budget for Joe R. Bush			
2					
3		Jan	Feb	Mar	1st Qtr
4					Total
5	Pension	2000	2000	2000	6000
6					
7	Expenses				
8	Mortgage	350	350	350	1050
9	Food	250	250	250	750
10	Utilities	150	150	150	450
11	Country C	350	350	350	1050
12	Miscellan	500	500	500	1500
13					
14	Total Expe	1600	1600	1600	4800
15					
16	Remainder	400	400	400	1200
17					

Adjusting column widths

When you entered the values, you may have noticed that some of the labels in column A were cut off when you typed in the values in column B. This is because the labels are too long for the default cell width provided by the program. The default cell width in Microsoft Excel 97 is 8.11 characters. Microsoft Excel 97 provides a command(s) to change the width of columns from 1 to 255 characters wide.

Two things to keep in mind about column widths. Data entered in as labels can spill into an adjacent cell, if that cell is empty. Should something be put into the adjacent cell, the label will be cut off (cut off from view only).

Values must always be contained in the cell into which they are typed. If a value is longer than the width of a cell, the Microsoft Excel 97 program will change the format (how it displays) to show ### or will make the value fit the cell width by changing it scientific notation.

Adjusting the Single column widths

🖑 Move the cell pointer to the column heading in column A.

🖑 Within the column heading of column A, move the pointer to the right edge and get the double arrow headed cross:

Double Click the left mouse button to size the **Column** automatically "best fit" to the largest item in the column.

Adjusting Multiple column widths

🖰 Move the cell pointer to the **Column Heading** in column B.

🖰 With the cell point as a large cross, hold the left mouse button down, and drag through column E.

The worksheet should look like the example below.

	B1			= Retirement Budget for Joe R. Bush		
A	B	C	D	E	F	C
	Retirement Budget for Joe R. Bush					
	Jan	Feb	Mar	1st Qtr Total		
Pension	2000	2000	2000	6000		
Expenses						
Mortgage	350	350	350	1050		
Food	250	250	250	750		
Utilities	150	150	150	450		
Country C	350	350	350	1050		
Miscellan	500	500	500	1500		
Total Expe	1600	1600	1600	4800		
Remainder	400	400	400	1200		

🖱 Within the column heading of any of one columns B to E move the pointer to the right edge and get the double arrow headed cross

🖱 Double Click the left mouse button to size the Columns automatically to "best fit" to the largest item in the column.

The worksheet should look like the example below.

	A	B	C	D	E	F
1		Retirement Budget for Joe R. Bush				
2						
3		Jan	Feb	Mar	1st Qtr	
4					Total	
5	Pension		2000	2000	2000	6000	
6						
7	Expenses					
8	Mortgage		350	350	350	1050	
9	Food		250	250	250	750	
10	Utilities		150	150	150	450	
11	Country C		350	350	350	1050	
12	Miscellan		500	500	500	1500	
13						
14	Total Expe		1600	1600	1600	4800	
15						
16	Remainder		400	400	400	1200	
17						
18						

Whoops, it really does not look like what we want. Column B is too big. Microsoft Excel 97 did what we asked. It sized the column to the largest item in each column. But what we asked for is not exactly what we wanted. So let's go fix it.

Moving the contents of a cell

First I would like for you to move the label in cell B1 to cell A1.

- ✍ Move to the worksheet title label in cell B1 to make it the current active cell.

- ✍ Put the mouse pointer on the edge of the bold cell border, to get a bold arrow, and hold the left mouse button down and drag to cell A1.

- ✍ When you move the pointer to A1, the contents will slide over. When you let go of the mouse button, the contents are moved.

This is what the screen should look like:

	A	B	C	D	E
1	Retirement	Budget for Joe R. Bush			
2					
3		Jan	Feb	Mar	1st Qtr
4					Total
5	Pension		2000	2000	2000	6000
6					
7	Expenses				

Merge and Center

Now we can center the worksheet title label across columns A through E.

- ✍ Make cell A1 as the current active cell

- ✍ Put the cell pointer in the middle of cell A1 and hold the mouse button down; then drag from cell A1 to E1, high-lighting the cells A1 to E1

- ✍ Release the mouse button

- ✍ Click on the Merge and Center button located on the Formatting toolbar. It looks like this

The worksheet should look like the example below.

A	B	C	D	E
Retirement Budget for Joe R. Bush				
	Jan	Feb	Mar	1st Qtr
				Total
Pension		2000	2000	2000	6000

Adjust the width of column B using the skills you've just learned adjusting the width of column A.

This is what the screen should look like after you've adjusted the width of column B:

A	B	C	D	E	F
Retirement Budget for Joe R. Bush					
	Jan	Feb	Mar	1st Qtr	
				Total	
Pension	2000	2000	2000	6000	
Expenses					
Mortgage	350	350	350	1050	
Food	250	250	250	750	
Utilities	150	150	150	450	
Country Club Dues	350	350	350	1050	
Miscellaneous	500	500	500	1500	
Total Expenses	1600	1600	1600	4800	
Remainder	400	400	400	1200	

Aligning Labels

Another format change needed is the alignment of the values and the column heading labels.

🖱 Move the cell pointer to cell B3, the cell that contains the **Jan** label.

🖱 With B3 as the current active cell, with the left mouse button down, drag to cell E4, highlighting cells B3 through E4 which contain the month labels and the total columns.

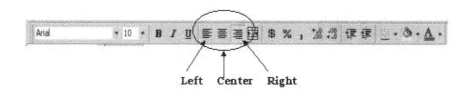

Left   Center   Right

Now you have three options to use to align your labels: **Left, Right** or **Center**. Left alignment will shift your label to the left edge of the column. Right alignment will shift your label to the right edge of the column. Center alignment will place the label in the middle of the column.

🖱 Select Center

This is what the screen should look like:

	Jan	Feb	Mar	1st Qtr Total
Budget for Joe R. Bush				
	2000	2000	2000	6000

Formatting Values

To add more appearance enhancements on the worksheet, you will now format the values relating to Pension, Total Expenses, and Remainder to a currency format. This will put dollar signs and commas into the number values. There is also an option to allow for the number of decimal places to be displayed. The rest of the values in the worksheet will be formatted as numbers with decimal places, but no dollar signs. Remember that the actual value does not change, just the display of the value.

🖰 Move the cell pointer to cell B5

This should be the top left value, number on the worksheet.

🖰 With B5 as the current active cell, put the cell pointer in the center of the cell and have the cell pointer as the large cross; hold the left mouse button down and drag to cell E16, highlighting cells B5 through E16.

Microsoft Excel 97 has many formatting options available. Each of these options will change the display of the value entries in a specified range.

🖰 Choose Format from the Main Menu.

🖰 Choose Cells from the Format menu.

🖰 The Format Cells dialog box shows the format choices allowed.

Screen showing highlighted cells and the cell formatting choices:

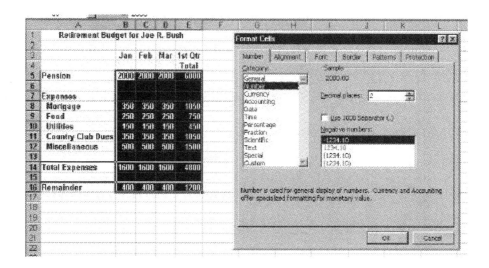

🖱 Click on the Number tab to bring it to the top

🖱 Click on Number, in the format choices.

🖱 Make sure that the Decimal places box is 2. Use the arrows on the side of the box to change them if needed.

🖱 Then click OK to format the range of cells we highlighted

Do not panic if the worksheet does not look exactly right, we will fix it in a few minutes. Please continue the lesson.

	A	B	C	D	E	F
1	Retirement Budget for Joe R. Bush					
2						
3		Jan	Feb	Mar	1st Qtr	
4					Total	
5	Pension	2000.00	2000.00	2000.00	6000.00	
6						
7	Expenses					
8	Mortgage	350.00	350.00	350.00	1050.00	
9	Food	250.00	250.00	250.00	750.00	
10	Utilities	150.00	150.00	150.00	450.00	
11	Country Club Dues	350.00	350.00	350.00	1050.00	
12	Miscellaneous	500.00	500.00	500.00	1500.00	
13						
14	Total Expenses	1600.00	1600.00	1600.00	4800.00	
15						
16	Remainder	400.00	400.00	400.00	1200.00	
17						

Formatting Non-Adjacent areas

Let's format the Pension, Total Expenses, and the Remainder rows to have dollar signs and commas.

🖰 Move the cell pointer to cell B5

🖰 With B5 as the current active cell, put the cell pointer in the center of the cell and have the cell pointer as the large cross; hold the left mouse button down and drag to cell E5, highlighting cells B5 through E5.

🖰 Hold down the Ctrl key

🖰 With the Ctrl key still down have the cell pointer as the large cross, move to cell B14 and hold the left mouse button down and drag to cell E14. Highlighting cells B14 through E14.

🖰 With the Ctrl key still down have the cell pointer as the large cross, move to cell B16 and hold the left mouse but-

ton down and drag to cell E16. Highlighting cells B14
through E14.

See the next example:

	A	B	C	D	E	F
1	Retirement Budget for Joe R. Bush					
2						
3		Jan	Feb	Mar	1st Qtr	
4					Total	
5	Pension	2000.00	2000.00	2000.00	6000.00	
6						
7	Expenses					
8	Mortgage	350.00	350.00	350.00	1050.00	
9	Food	250.00	250.00	250.00	750.00	
10	Utilities	150.00	150.00	150.00	450.00	
11	Country Club Dues	350.00	350.00	350.00	1050.00	
12	Miscellaneous	500.00	500.00	500.00	1500.00	
13						
14	Total Expenses	1600.00	1600.00	1600.00	4800.00	
15						
16	Remainder	400.00	400.00	400.00	1200.00	
17						
18						

⌐ With three rows highlighted format these values to
   Currency 2 decimal places. Use the same method you
   learned earlier in this lesson to complete this formatting

The worksheet should look like the example below, but if it does
not, we will fix it in a few minutes. Please continue with the lesson.

B16	▼	= =B5-B14				
	A	B	C	D	E	F
1		Retirement Budget for Joe R. Bush				
2						
3		Jan	Feb	Mar	1st Qtr	
4					Total	
5	Pension	$ 2,000.00	$ 2,000.00	$ 2,000.00	$ 6,000.00	
6						
7	Expenses					
8	Mortgage	350.00	350.00	350.00	1050.00	
9	Food	250.00	250.00	250.00	750.00	
10	Utilities	150.00	150.00	150.00	450.00	
11	Country Club Dues	350.00	350.00	350.00	1050.00	
12	Miscellaneous	500.00	500.00	500.00	1500.00	
13						
14	Total Expenses	$ 1,600.00	$ 1,600.00	$ 1,600.00	$ 4,800.00	
15						
16	Remainder	$ 400.00	$ 400.00	$ 400.00	$ 1,200.00	
17						
18						

If your worksheet looks something like the following example, here is how to fix it:

	Retirement Budget for Joe R. Bush			
	Jan	Feb	Mar	1st Qtr
				Total
Pension	#####	#####	#####	#####
Expenses				
Mortgage	#####	#####	#####	#####
Food	#####	#####	#####	#####
Utilities	#####	#####	#####	#####
Country Club Dues	#####	#####	#####	#####
Miscellaneous	#####	#####	#####	#####
Total Expenses	#####	#####	#####	#####
Remainder	#####	#####	#####	#####

Remember if a value, a number, is too large to fit in a cell, it shows either in Scientific Notation or as # signs. The problem is, we need to adjust the column widths for columns B through E. Do you remember how to do this from earlier in the lesson? If not,

🖰 Move the cell pointer to the **Column Heading** in column B.

🖰 With the cell point as a large cross ✛ hold the left mouse button down and drag to column E.

🖰 Within the column heading of any one column, B to E, move the pointer to the right edge and get the double arrow headed cross

🖰 Double Click the left mouse button to size the **Columns** automatically "best fit" to the largest item in the column.

Now the worksheet should look like the example below.

A	B	C	D	E
Retirement Budget for Joe R. Bush				
	Jan	Feb	Mar	1st Qtr Total
Pension	$2,000.00	$2,000.00	$2,000.00	$6,000.00
Expenses				
Mortgage	350.00	350.00	350.00	1050.00
Food	250.00	250.00	250.00	750.00
Utilities	150.00	150.00	150.00	450.00
Country Club Dues	350.00	350.00	350.00	1050.00
Miscellaneous	500.00	500.00	500.00	1500.00
Total Expenses	$1,600.00	$1,600.00	$1,600.00	$4,800.00
Remainder	$ 400.00	$ 400.00	$ 400.00	$1,200.00

Changing Fonts

Now we need to change the Font on the worksheet. To do this easily, let's use the Select All Button.

🖱 Click on the button or small box above the row 1's heading and to the left of column A.

When you click there the worksheet will look like the example below, all black.

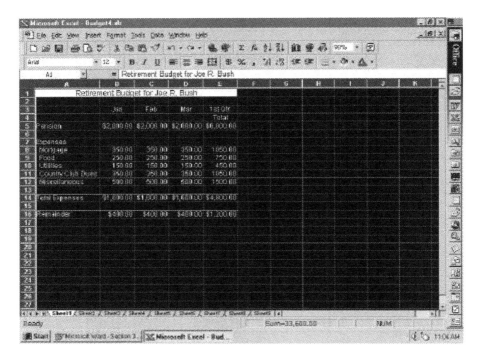

🖱 Now move the mouse pointer up to Font Box and choose Times New Roman and click to choose that Font type.

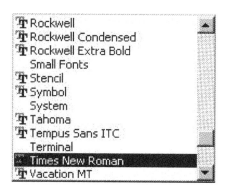

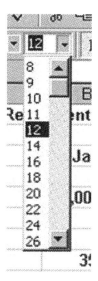

Move the mouse pointer to the Font Size box next to the Font Box and choose 12.

Adjust the column widths if needed.

Move to Cell A1 to make it the current active cell; that is where the worksheet title is located on the worksheet. Change the font to 18.

Remember the center across columns. This makes the title look like it is not in cell A1. If you look in the Formula Bar while cell A1 is the current active cell you can see the actual contents.

🖰 Then click on the Bold Button **B** to bold the label.

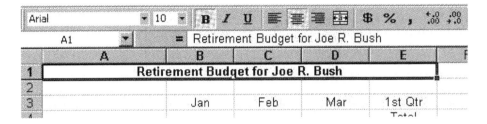

You have done a lot of work,

🖰 Save your workbook now.

Printing a worksheet

Printing allows us to get a hard copy, a printed copy, of the worksheet.

🖰 Choose **File** from the Main Menu.

🖰 Select **Print** from the File menu. The following dialog box will display:

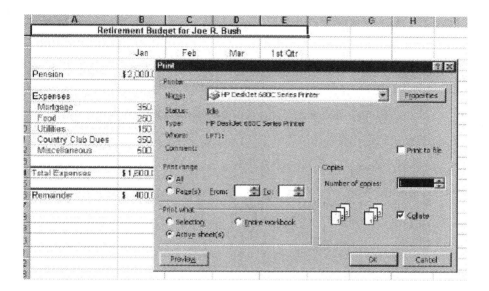

You may notice that there are several options here; you can:

❖ Change printers

❖ Decide on what to print, a selected portion of a work-sheet, a single worksheet, or the whole workbook.

❖ Set page range allows you to print specific pages from a large worksheet if it has several pages.

❖ You may also print multiple copies of a page(s).

🖰 Without making any changes in the dialog box, Click on OK to print.

Things to Remember

Terms

Define or explain the meaning, usage, or how-to of each of the following terms:

Adjusting column widths

Single Column

Multiple Columns

Formatting

Labels

Bold

Underline

Italic

Font

Font Size

Justification

left

right

center

Center Across Columns

Values

Currency

Commas

Decimal Point

Printing

The Worksheet

The Workbook

Specified Cells

Lines and Borders

LESSON 22
GRAPHICS

Now that you've formatted your budget worksheet, in this lesson you will:

❖ Make a **pie chart**, which provides a comparison of data

❖ Print the chart

❖ Save the chart to a disk for merging later into your word processing document

All spreadsheet programs generally include the ability to produce high-quality presentation graphics or charts. Microsoft Excel 97 produces excellent charts and graphs. Charts and graphs provide an opportunity to display the data in an easy to understand "picture." They can be used to emphasize a particular point by providing a comparison of various chart objects.

Spreadsheets usually produce line, bar, pie and area charts in 2 or 3D. Microsoft Excel 97 creates all of these and many more. Each of these types of charts shows either a trend or provides a comparison, or both. Microsoft Excel 97 has the capability to create, save and print graphs.

🖰 Retrieve the BUDGET worksheet from your disk. See the figure below.

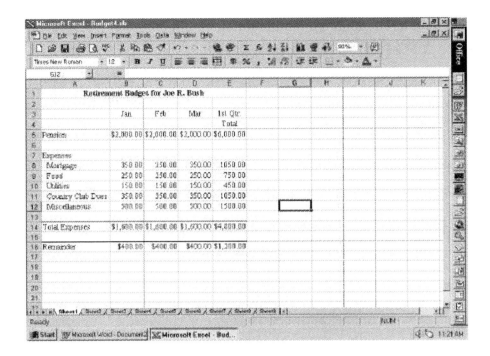

Charts are produced from a series, or several series of data values.

In this lesson, you will be using the Budget worksheet we created in an earlier lesson to make a pie chart. This pie chart will compare each Item to the Expense item's total in the "1st Qtr Total". Another way to say it is that we will compare column A with column, column E as a whole. If you don't quite get it should make sense later. If not as your instructor.

🖱 Move the cell pointer to cell **A8**.

🖱 Hold the left mouse button down and drag down, highlighting through **A12**.

🖱 Hold down the **Ctrl** key.

🖱 With the Ctrl key down, click on Cell **E8**.

✍ Hold the left mouse button down and drag down, high-lighting through **E12**.

This is what the screen should look like:

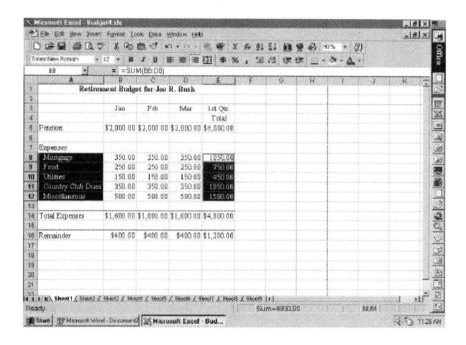

✍ Click on the **Chart Wizard** button located on the Standard Toolbar (as shown in the next figure. The Chart Wizard dialog box will display, it looks like the figure below.

Chart Wizard

☝ Select **Pie** from the list of Chart types.

As you can see, there are several types of charts for you to choose from. You need to carefully consider the chart type you use. Charts show data graphically. The chart type needs to match the data and how the data is best displayed to convey the idea you want to get across.

Within Pie charts are several types of pie charts, as shown in the following graphic:

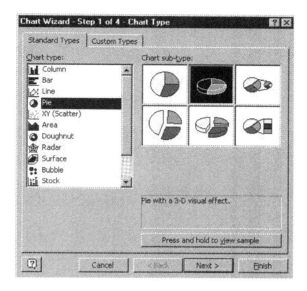

🖱 Click on 3D pie. The one highlighted in the example above.

🖱 Click next.

Your screen should look like the example below.

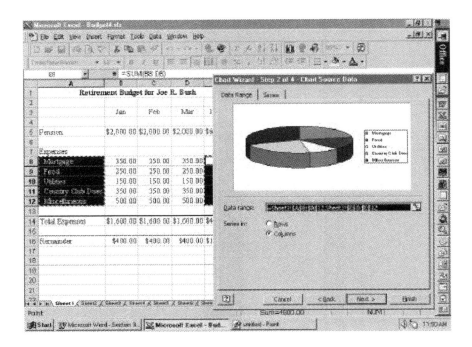

The sample chart in the Chart Wizard box shows you what the chart will look like if you were to click on the finish button, but we have some more work to do.

- Click next.

- Choose the title tab, if it is not the current tab.

- Type in your worksheet's title. "Retirement Budget for Joe R. Bush".

- Click the Legend tab

- Make sure that show legend does **not** have check mark.

- Click the Data Labels tab

- Choose Show Label and Percent

🖱 Click next

🖱 Choose the option of Object in: This sets the chart to appear as a part of your worksheet.

🖱 Click Finish

The completed pie chart should look like the example below.

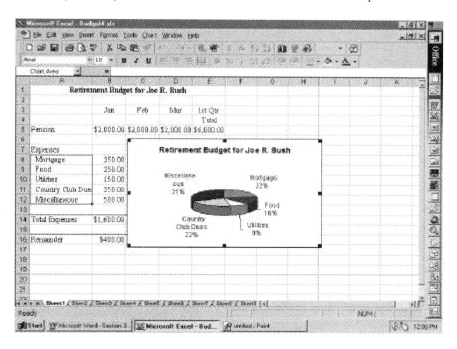

Most likely, the chart is not exactly where you would like it displayed as a part of your worksheet.

🖱 To move the chart put your pointer on any of the white space in the chart and hold the left mouse button down and drag the chart.

🖱 Place the top left corner in cell A18 and release the mouse.

Your worksheet should now look like the example below.

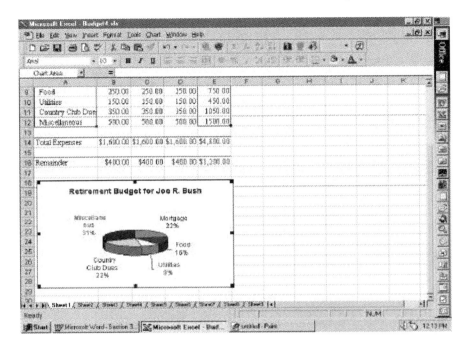

Types of Charts

In addition to the pie chart, there are several other types of charts you can create in Microsoft Excel. The other types of charts are listed along with the pie chart on the Chart Wizard Chart types list:

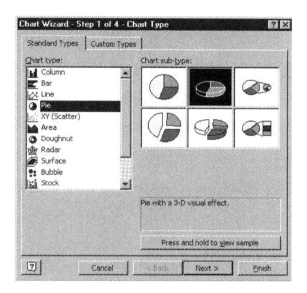

Some of the most commonly used types of charts, and what they are used to show, are:

❖ Column charts   A column chart is used to compare amounts that represent different time, entities, or events. Like the number of "A" grades given in Computer Literacy for each quarter.

❖ Bar charts   A bar chart is very similar to a column chart except it measures how long or how much of something usually against time. The total number of each grade in a quarter (which each grade having its own bar).

❖ Line charts   A line chart tracks multiple values for something by connecting the various values on a line. For instance, the price of disks for the past two years with a price plotted on the charted for each month. The line would connect the dots to show the trend line.

❖ The other chart types have special uses and functions. If you are curious, visit Excel help and look each up for an explanation of its use.

🖑 Save the worksheet. This will save the worksheet and the attached chart.

🖑 Print the worksheet and attached pie chart.

This concludes your introduction to electronic spreadsheets and Microsoft Excel 97. Spreadsheets are extremely valuable tools for much beyond the lessons in this book. If you have further interest, ask your instructor to recommend additional spreadsheet courses.

Things to Remember

TERMS
Explain, define, or describe the use, action, or purpose of each of the following chart terms:

Chart Type

      Pie

      Bar

      Column

3-D Pie

Chart Area

Chart Wizard

Legend

SECTION 4

COMPLETING THE DOCUMENT

In this section, you will perform the task to finish your research report document. In the following lessons, you will:

- ❖ do Internet research
- ❖ create a works cited page
- ❖ perform spelling and grammar checking
- ❖ insert a table and a graph
- ❖ add headers and footers
- ❖ insert research materials
- ❖ edit your document from a proofreader's page
- ❖ add a cover page

LESSON 23
INTERNET RESEARCH

In Lesson 6 you had an introduction research. This included the Internet and an opportunity to try out some of the Internet components and features.

In this section we will:

* ❖ Review the parts of the Internet

* ❖ Learn how to better use web browsers

* ❖ Learn how to use a search engine

* ❖ Use the Internet to find specific information

* ❖ Find data to create a small section of text to add to FULLTERM.DOC

* ❖ Learn how to give credit to an Internet source

The Internet is sometimes referred to as the information highway. The Internet is made up of many separate networks of computers connected together by several different types of devices. These devices range from LAN, a Local Area Network, modems, phone lines, fiber optic cables, to satellites in space. All this allows worldwide communication in moments.

Because the Internet is made up of many networks, it requires us to gain access to it. For a user to access the Internet he must get connected to it. You could use a computer at the public library, a friend's, or use your own computer at home.

To get your computer connected to the Internet you must have hardware (the computer) and a modem or a LAN connection. Once you have all this you need to get a service provider to provide the connection from your modem or LAN to the Internet. There are many Internet service providers, including American On Line, CompuServe Prodigy, Microsoft Network, or many small private local service providers. The cost of Internet access varies among service providers. Cost also depends upon the services you want and how much you use the service(s) you subscribe to. The costs now range from $10.00 to $35.00 a month or more. Remember service providers are very competitive, and the costs and services will change quickly. If you plan to use the Internet and you are not connected, choose a service provider with technical support to help you get the correct hardware and software get set up.

Now that you are connected, let's talk about some of the specific features or services of the Internet.

E-mail, or Electronic Mail, is correspondence between one or more users on a network or through the Internet. An e-mail message is essentially a letter or memo sent electronically from one user to one or more others. Typically, networks and Internet service providers will provide e-mail.

File Transfer Protocol, FTP, is a method for moving or transferring files from one computer to another on the Internet. The files can contain software, text, graphics, sound, animation, or video. Usually the transfer takes place to or from a host computer to your microcomputer. The host has data and programs centrally located so the users of the network can access them.

Gopher is a menu driven Internet service that helps you locate information. You connect through a host computer called a Gopher Server. Using Gopher is easy; the Gopher Server shows you a list of options and you select the one you want. Many of these options will link you to other Gopher sites.

Newsgroups or Usenet is an Internet service that maintains thousands of discussion groups involving millions of people all over the world. Usually each discussion group focuses on a particular topic such as computers, cars, food, travel, and so on. Some groups are single-topic-only groups. Others may be formal and structured, or informal, with varied subjects.

Telnet is a computer program that lets you connect to a host computer anywhere on the Internet and use your computer just as if you were using a terminal directly attached to that network's host. A host computer is a computer on a network. Most networks require user accounts and passwords for security. When you telnet to a site and attempt to connect you will probably be required to have an account and password. Some Telnet sites may allow an anonymous account and password which lets anyone log on. Networks have high security and rights to only specific areas of the network. These network rights are given to users by their account name. Anonymous users may have very limited accounts and access to data and areas of the network.

World Wide Web, Web (WWW) is a service on the Internet, which presents information in a well organized and accessible format. It often includes multimedia--sound, video, animation, and graphics. Some of the best and most easily accessible information in the Internet is available through the Web covering almost every conceivable subject. The Web consists of pages, called Web pages containing information on a particular subject. In addition to the available information on the current page, the page may include links that point to other places on that page or other pages on other computers connected on the Internet. To access Web information, "Surf the Net", you will need access to the Internet and a Web Browser software that displays the text, graphics, sound, video, and animation for a Web page. Some of the most popular Web Browsers are Netscape and Microsoft Internet Explorer.

In Lesson 6 you learned some basic features about Internet. Use what you have learned in the following lesson.

🖰 Open your Web browser

You should have the instructions written down in lesson 6 from your instructor. In this exercise we will use Microsoft Internet Explorer. It will only be similar to the example below because your start up home page may be different than the example. In this lesson we are using the Microsoft Internet start page located at the URL http://home.microsoft.com/. (Remember that a Web Browser is software, which displays the text, graphics, sound, video, and animation for a Web page.) Below is a picture of the Walla Walla Community College start page, also called a home page. Your start page will probably be different.

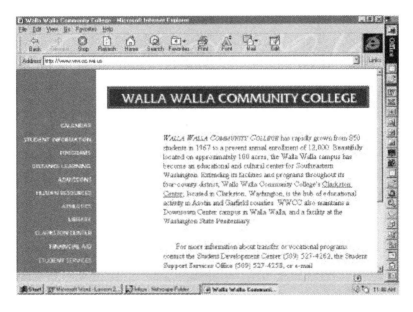

Now that we are on the Internet, "The Net," and we have a Web Browser running we can search the net, or "Surf The Net," for some needed information. One of the objectives of this lesson is to find data and add it to the FULLTERM.DOC file.

So how can we easily do that?

One way to effectively surf the net is to use a Search Engine. Search Engines are really indexes of available Web pages. They are databases containing the URLs, (Uniform Resource Locator or the Internet address of the page), and a title and a brief description of the data each contain. To access any good Search Engine available, we need only type in the URL for the Search Engine at the address line of the Web Browser.

Listed below are three of our favorite search engines and their URLs:

AltaVista	http://www.altavista.digital.com
Lycos	http://www/lycos.com
Yahoo	http://www/yahoo.com
Excite	http://www.excite.com

Or, we can use the search button built into the browser or use favorites already saved into the software.

☞ Type http://www/excite.com in the address box and enter.

See the example below:

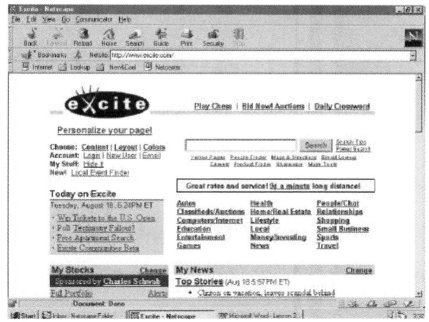

🖰 Type the URL for each search engine suggested above and save them with the Favorite button, (for MS Explorer), or the Bookmark button, (for Netscape).

Remember that the Internet is very dynamic and is changing continuously; therefore, your results from searches and screens will probably look somewhat different than these examples.

Now let's see if we can find some information that we can use to finish this lesson. Remember that we need to find data to create a paragraph to add to the FULLTERM.DOC file.

🖰 Get the search engine Excite loaded into the browser

🖰 Type in Retirement Planning in the search box, next to the Search button.

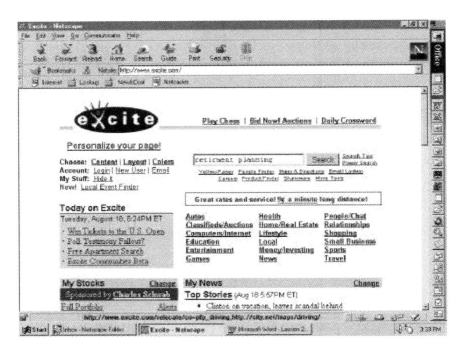

🖱 **C**lick on the Search button to start the search

Notice below in our search that Excite found lot's of items and listed them by how strongly they match the query. The best matches are first. We do not want to look at all these, so let's see if we can get a little closer to a reasonable number to read.

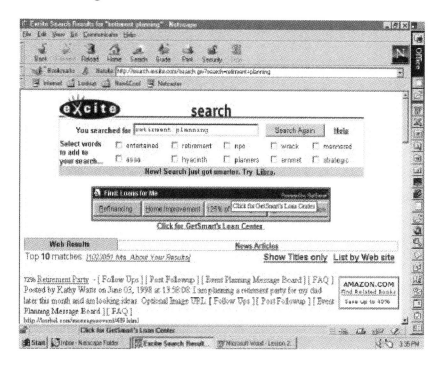

Look down through the list of possible sites Excite is showing. Usually there are 10 to 20 showing on each page.

🖱 At the bottom of the page click on "Power Search" to refine the search.

It should look like the following example:

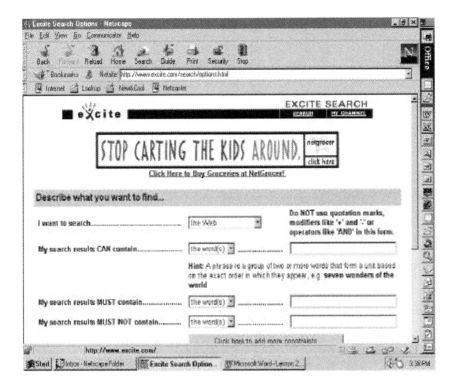

⊕ Click in the box "My search MUST contain" and type in the word "Retirement" and enter.

⊕ Then click on "Click here to add more constraints."

⊕ Make sure the down arrow boxes have "Must Contain"

⊕ Then add the word "Planning" in the next box.

⊕ Add one more constraint box and "Must Contain"

⊕ Then type in the word "Tips"

See the example below:

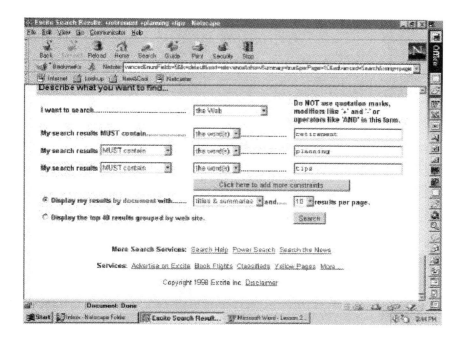

🐭 Click on "Search"

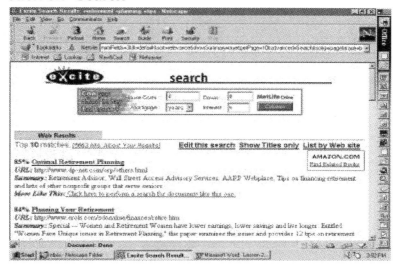

Now you can choose one of the web pages suggested by the Excite search engine, by reading the summary to see if it is appropriate for your needs.

Remember the documents and the number of documents you find may be different than mine because the Web is so dynamic and changes all the time.

Each page suggested has a short description and a link to its URL.

☞ Take some time to look at all the relevant documents that you found. Each Web page will probably have links built within the page to take you to other places within that page, or to other pages. When you find something of interest, print the information.

Remember that the Internet is very dynamic and is changing continuously; therefore, your results from searches and screens will look somewhat different than these examples.

You are looking for data to create a short paragraph to add to the FULLTERM.DOC file.

☞ Use the results of your research to compose a paragraph on paper to insert into the FULLTERM file in a future lesson.

Since you have researched the Web and printed out some interesting data pertinent to retirement, you need to give credit to the Internet source you used. You will create a reference for the Work Cited page to give credit to the source of the data.

Referencing On-line or Electronic sources is relatively new, and an exact standard has not completely emerged. The goal is to give credit to the author/source and to give the reader of your paper the ability to find your material to do further reading or research.

For this project, use the following example and adapt it to the document you found.

Our search results would be something like:

> College Board On Line. (1997). Financial Planning Tips.[Excite] Financial Aid Services. <u>Available</u>: http://www.collegeboard.org/css/html/plantip.html

The reference form gives:

> Author or source,
>
> Date (1997) or (1997, June 15).
>
> Title of the document or article.
>
> The search engine or Internet feature used. (Lycos, or FTP etc.).

The name of the periodical, journal, or service from which the document came. (Make sure this title is underlined.) Notice that the commas and periods are bold to help you remember. The punctuation is extremely important. This style may vary, depending on what information is available. Ask your instructor for specific help if needed.

Things to Remember

TERMS

> AltaVista
>
> AOL
>
> CompuServe
>
> E-mail
>
> FTP
>
> Gopher

Internet Provider

LAN, a Local Area Network

Lycos

Microsoft Explorer

Modem

Netscape

Newsgroups

Prodigy

Service Provider

Telnet

Usenet

Web Browser

WWW

Yahoo

LESSON 24
WORKS CITED PAGE

In this lesson you are going to type the Works Cited page of your research paper. The Works Cited page will be located on a separate page at the end of your paper and contain the references used in the paper with the proper MLA format, using underline and center commands where needed.

🖰 Use the steps you've learned to open the FULLTERM document.

Move the cursor to the very end of the document. There are several ways of reaching the end of a document:

Method 1: Hold down the **down arrow** key until you have scrolled through the whole document (very slow method).

Method 2: Press the **PgDn** key until you have progressed through all the pages (a window at a time) until you reach the end of the document (slow).

Method 3: While holding down the **Ctrl** key press the **End** key. Word will position the cursor at the end of the document (fast).

(If you have extra Enters, Tabs, spaces, etc., at the end of your document, the cursor will be after these items.)

🖰 Choose one of the methods to move to the bottom of the FULLTERM document.

🖰 If you have extra commands after the text, clean them out by using the delete key.

This is what the bottom of your document should look like:

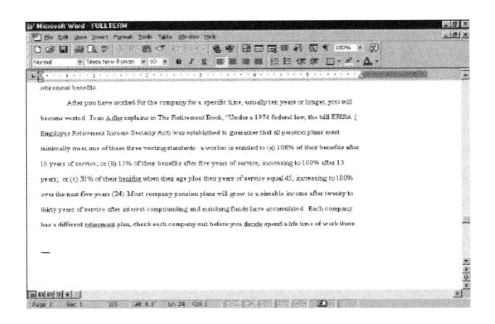

Inserting a Manual or Hard Page Break

Now you need to put in a page break so you can type the Works Cited page on what will be the last page of your document.

Remember that the program automatically puts soft page breaks in your document when you've filled a page with text (default setting).

You can manually insert page breaks whenever you want to force a page break at a particular spot. When you force page breaks they're called hard page breaks. In Word when a hard page break is inserted the cursor jumps to the top of a new page.

When you insert a hard page break, Word will put soft page breaks in any following text where needed.

To insert a hard page break from the menu:

- ☜ Click on **Insert** in the Menu bar
- ☜ Select **Break**
- ☜ Select **Page Break**
- ☜ Choose **OK**

OR

Insert a hard page break from the keyboard:

- ☜ While holding down the **Ctrl** key press the **ENTER** key

If you accidentally put a hard page break in the wrong place use the following steps to delete it, then go back and try again.

- ☜ Move the cursor to the end of the line of text where the hard page break was inserted and press the **Delete** key

Remember that you want a hard page break after the last paragraph in the FULLTERM document.

Next you will be creating the text known as the Works Cited page that is needed for the research paper you have been working with.

When you type the Works Cited page, use the center and underline commands you've learned in previous lessons. If you don't remember, go back and review the steps or use the Help feature to review.

When typing a sentence or reference containing a colon (:), type two spaces after the colon.

When typing a reference, each reference should end with the ENTER key. A reference is looked at as a paragraph.

- ☜ Type the following text as your Works Cited page using center and underline where needed:

Works Cited

Adler, Joan. The Retirement Book. New York: William Morrow and Company, Inc., 1975.

Burchell, Robert W. "Urban America". Center for Urban Policy Research, Rutgers University 1991.

Dickinson, Peter A. The Complete Retirement Planning Book. New York: E.P. Dutton, 1976.

Gibbs, Nancy R. "Greys on the Go." Time 22 Feb. 1988: 66.

Jacobs, Sheldon. "Retirement Planning Strategies." Investment Vision March/April, 1989: 9.

Lulevitch, Tom. "I.R.A.'s." Investment Vision March/April, 1989: 2-4.

Page, Cynthia L. Your Retirement. New York: Arco, 1984.

Stinnett, Nick, at al. Relationships in Marriage and the Family. New York: Macmillan, 1984.

Tiffany, Richard. Personal Interview. 19 Feb. 1991.

Weber, Louis. "Your Retirement: Company and Private Pensions." Consumer Guide. New York: 1981

This is what the top of the Works Cited page should look like:

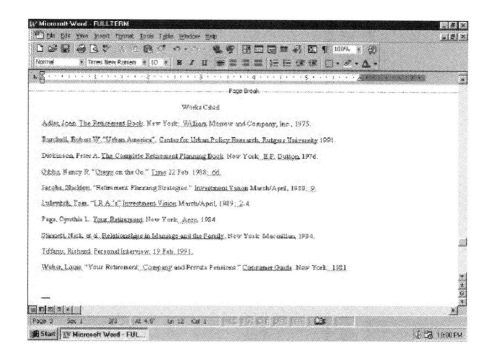

🖰 When you have completed the Works Cited page having done any needed editing, resave the document with the same name (FULLTERM).

Printing a Selected Page

Now let's print only the Works Cited page of the document.

🖰 Place the cursor somewhere on the Works Cited page of the FULLTERM document.

🖰 Click on **File** in the Menu bar

🖰 Click on **Print**

🖰 Select **Current Page**

This is what the print menu will look like with Current Page selected:

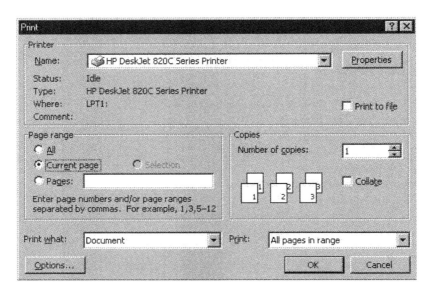

↸ Click **OK**

Turn this page in to your instructor if it is requested.

↸ Close your FULLTERM document and Exit Word

Things to Remember

1. Give the purpose, function or meaning of each of the following:

Ctrl + End

Ctrl + ENTER

Center

Underline

2. How many spaces are there after a colon?

3. How do you print one page only?

4. What is a hard page break?

LESSON 25
SPELLING & GRAMMAR

In this lesson you are going to learn to use the Spelling and Grammar Checking feature of Word 97 to check your TERM1 and FULLTERM documents for errors.

It is a good idea to make sure your document has been saved before using the Spelling and Grammar Checker. If you had made changes to the document you would want to save it before you checked it.

For this lesson you will be shown a copy of the TERM1 document that contains some misspelled words. Your document is probably perfect, so won't contain these misspelled words.

☝ Open the TERM1 document from your disk, using steps previously learned.

The Spelling and Grammar Checker checks your document for spelling errors using the Word dictionary and grammar errors using a set of English grammar rules. If the word isn't found in the dictionary it is displayed in the Spelling dialog box with an indicating message. The word may not be misspelled. If the word is a proper name, abbreviation, or specialized term the dictionary will not recognize it. If you type the word from' instead of form' or if' instead of is' the Spell Checker will not pick this up; these words are correctly spelled but in the wrong context. Mistakes like this must be found when you proof your document by carefully reading through it.

If the word is misspelled, the Word dictionary will look for choices offering possible correct spellings for you to choose from.

The Grammar Checker goes through your document looking for grammar errors. Like the Spell Checker it doesn't recognize proper names, abbreviations, or punctuation in your Works

Cited page. As the Grammar Checker goes through your document you must decide if the suggested changes are needed; not all of the changes are right for your document.

Throughout your lessons you have created TERM1 and FULL-TERM documents, either typing the text yourself or bringing it in from the TERM2 document. As you typed, you fixed the obvious mistakes. The Spell Checker will help you find spelling errors that you may have missed. The Grammar Checker will help you with grammar errors.

When you invoke (start) Word's Spelling and Grammar Checker, it checks your whole document.

Now let's check the TERM1 document first.

🖰 Use one of the methods you've learned to position the cursor at the top of the document

🖰 Point to the Spelling and Grammar button on the Standard toolbar; Click

If the word middle in middle aged is misspelled the screen should look like this:

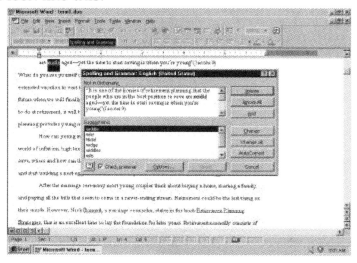

Word will begin checking the spelling at the top of the document. When a word is not found in the dictionary it will be displayed in a dialog box. If the word shows up in the dialog box, but is correct, you want to Ignore it. If the word is a proper name which you want to **ignore** throughout the document, use **Ignore All.**

If the word is actually misspelled:

In this case the word **midle** is misspelled. The correct spelling is **middle** which is the computer's most logical choice, and so is highlighted. If you wanted one of the other choices you would point to your choice and click.

Since we want the spelling **middle**, which is already highlighted:

🖑 Click on the **Change** button. The spelling of the word is immediately changed.

The program will go on to the next misspelled word or grammar error.

The next problem detected is a grammar error. The words **What ever** in the sentence the book had you insert should be combined into one word, **Whatever**.

This is what the screen should look like:

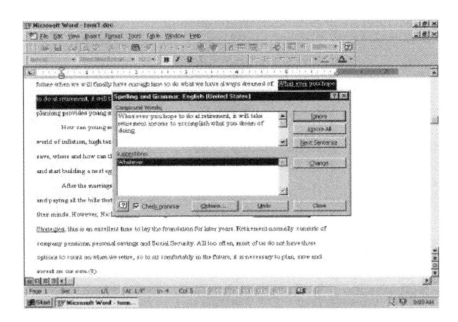

🖰 Click on the **Change** button. The spelling of the word is immediately changed and follows proper grammar rules.

The next error found is a grammar error but you will ignore it. The editing lesson coming up will have you fix this problem.

This is what your screen should look like:

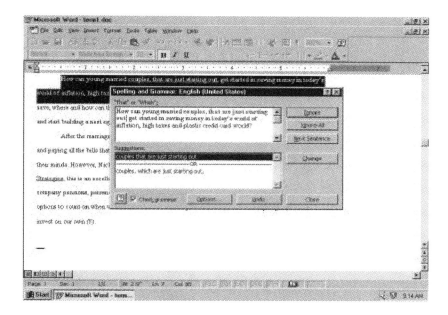

🖱 Point to either the **Ignore** button; Click.

The program will go on to the next misspelled word or grammar. In this case it is a proper name, **Stinnett**. Since this is the correct spelling and the word occurs again later in the document, you would want to choose **Ignore All**.

This is what your screen should look like:

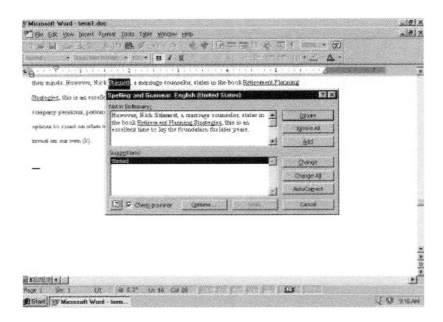

If the word is not misspelled, choose one of the following:

🖱 Point to either the **Ignore** or **Ignore All** button, whichever pertains to the situation; Click.

When the Spelling and Grammar Checker has gone through your whole document and has dealt with the problems (correcting or ignoring), the screen will show the following message:

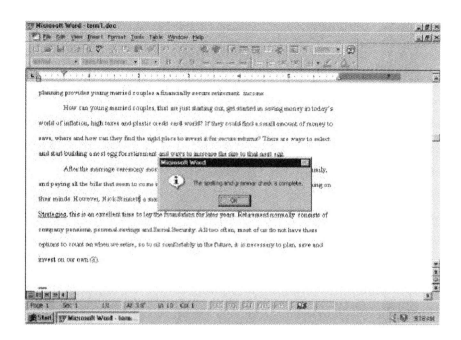

To leave the Spelling and Grammar Checker:

🖰 Point to the **OK** button; Click

🖰 Since you have corrected the spelling and grammar throughout the document be sure that you resave the document with the changes you have made.

🖰 Close the TERM1 document.

Since the FULLTERM document is the document that you are currently working with you should check the spelling and grammar.

*** As you proceed through the FULLTERM document ignore the grammar errors at this time. You will check the document for grammar errors again after you have made editing changes in lesson 29.

⌐ **Open** the FULLTERM document and run the **Spelling and Grammar Checker**

Once you have checked for spelling errors in the FULLTERM document:

⌐ **Close** the FULLTERM document and **Exit** Word

Things to Remember

1. How does the Spell Checker react to:

a. misspelled words?

b. proper names?

c. abbreviations?

d. specialized terms?

LESSON 26
TABLES & GRAPHS

In this lesson, you will merge the worksheet and chart created in Excel into the FULLTERM document. The worksheet and pie chart will be placed at the beginning of a page in the text.

Tables, charts, and graphics can add clarity to a narrative as well as giving the document more impact.

🖰 Open Word for Windows

🖰 Open the FULLTERM document

🖰 Move the cursor to the end of the first paragraph on page 2.

The paragraph begins "To be comfortable when you retire," Be sure you are at the end of the paragraph, right behind the period. Use the **End** key to position the cursor once you are on the correct line.

This is what your document should look like after these steps:

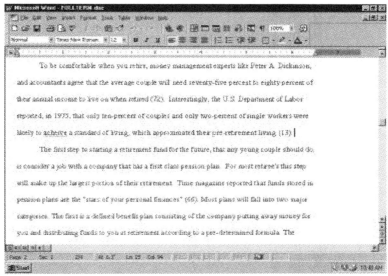

🖑 Press the **ENTER** key to start a new paragraph. This is where you insert your worksheet and graph.

This is what the screen should look like:

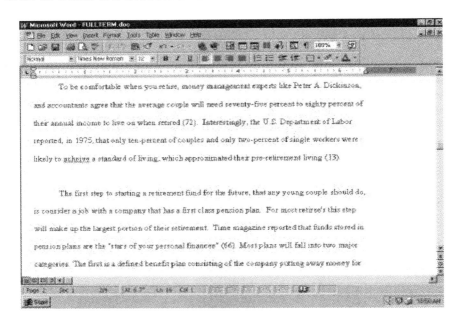

Since Word and Excel are both Windows application programs, the worksheet and pie chart that you created in Excel can be placed in your Word document easily.

Inserting a worksheet and chart

With the cursor sitting at the left margin on the blank line you inserted after the paragraph:

🖑 Click on **Insert** in the Menu toolbar

🖑 Click on **Object**

🖑 Click on **Create from File**

🖱 Click on File Name window box, Delete the *.*

🖱 Type in the path and filename of the worksheet you created in previous lessons
(A:\SPREADSHEETS\BUDGET.XLS)

This is what the screen should look like:

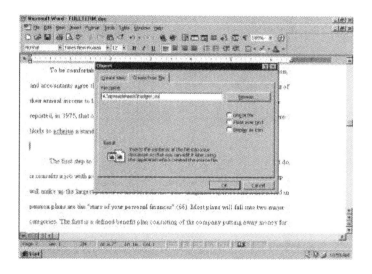

🖱 Click on **OK**

🖱 Press the **Up arrow** key to show the end of the previous paragraph and the spreadsheet

Your screen should look similar to the one shown, and should contain your own name in the title.

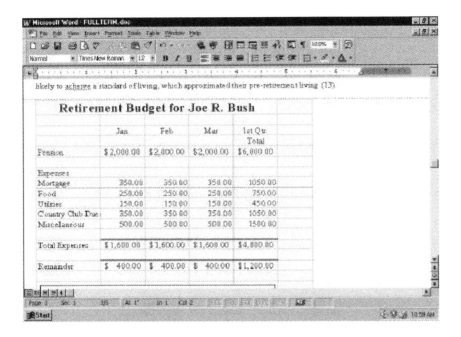

Centering and Editing the Worksheet on the page

🖰 Point anywhere on the worksheet

🖰 Click the right mouse button

🖰 Move the pointer down to **Worksheet Object**

🖰 Move the pointer right to **Edit**

This is what the screen should look like when the worksheet is active:

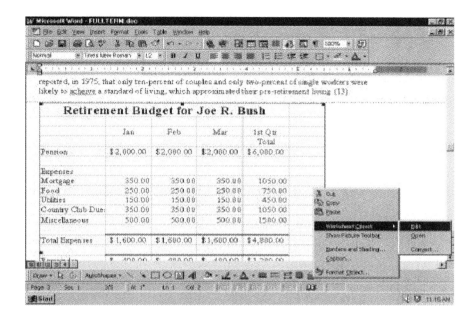

✏️ Click on **Edit**

✏️ Point to the center handle on the right side of the worksheet. When the mouse pointer changes from the **+** cross to an arrow pointing in both directions « , hold down the left mouse button and drag to the left until any blank columns are gone. Be careful that you don't lose any of the columns that contain values.

✏️ Move the pointer outside of the worksheet; Click to deactivate Excel

This is what your screen should look like:

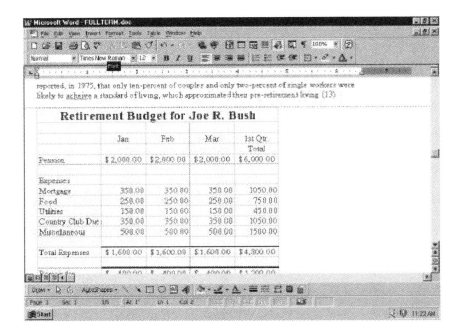

🖱 Click once anywhere on the worksheet to make it active in Word

🖱 Point to the **Center** button in the Formatting toolbar; Click

🖱 Arrow up once to see the end of the previous paragraph

Your screen should now look like the following graphic:

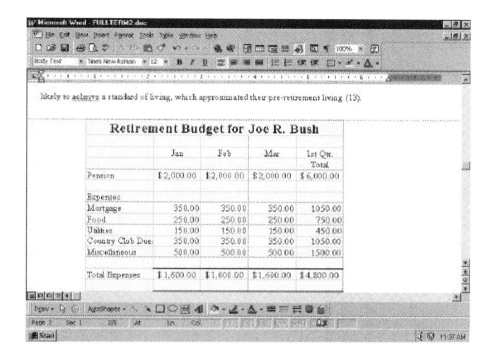

The Worksheet is now centered on the page. **GOOD JOB**!

If your document doesn't look like the one displayed, go back and figure out what is wrong and fix it. If things seem so messed up that you don't think you can fix them, close the document without saving and reopen your original FULLTERM document. Go through the steps in this lesson again to insert the worksheet.

When you have the document looking the way you want with the worksheet inserted:

🖑 Resave your FULLTERM document

🖑 Exit Word

LESSON 27
HEADERS & FOOTERS

In this lesson you are going to learn about headers, footers, and page numbering. Headers are lines of text that appear at the top of every page of printed output within the top margin. Footers are lines of text that appear at the bottom of every printed page within the bottom margin.

Headers and footers usually contain information that you want repeated on every page, like a page number, date, your name, or chapter number and title.

Headers and footers can be formatted like any other part of the document, but are usually positioned within the page's top and bottom margins. Word for Windows will allow you to place headers and footers anywhere on the page.

When headers and footers are created and edited, Word switches you to the page layout view and displays headers and footers at the top or bottom of the page, just as they appear when the document is printed.

Remember that a header is text that you want printed at the top of every page. A footer is text you want printed at the bottom of every page. Both are printed within the top or bottom margins.

You want your cursor at the top of the document when creating a header or footer.

- ✋ Open Word for Windows
- ✋ Open the FULLTERM document

Create a Header

Now let's create a header in your FULLTERM document that shows your last name and a page number in the top right corner of the page.

🖑 Place the cursor in the left topmost corner of the document using steps you've learned

🖑 Click **View** in the Menu bar

Your screen should look like this:

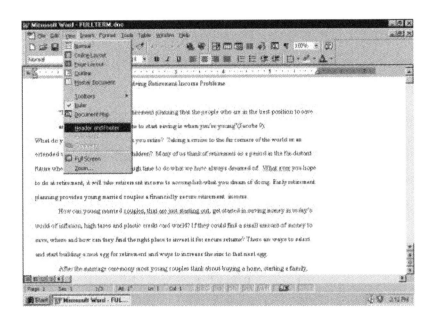

🖑 Select **Header and Footer**

Another screen is displayed, the header screen:

Your research paper requires a header containing your last name, all in capital letters, and the page number. These are to be displayed on the far right of the page.

🖰 Point to the **Right Align** button in the Formatting toolbar; Click
The cursor will jump to the right side of the header area (flush right)

🖰 Type your last name all in capital letters, then press the spacebar once

🖰 Point to the **Page Number** button in the Header/Footer toolbar; Click

This is what your screen should look like:

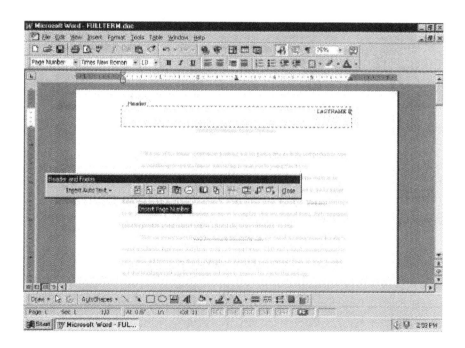

This finishes your header.

🖰 Click on the **Close** button in the Header/Footer toolbar

Research papers require that the header containing your name and the page number NOT print on the first page, but print on all other pages.

Suppress the Header on the first page

8 Click on **Insert** in the Menu bar

8 Select **Page Numbers**

This is what your screen should look like:

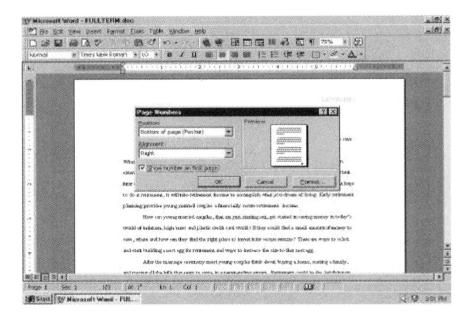

You want to turn off the default setting showing numbers on first page.

◌ Click on the **Show Number on First Page** box to turn the header off on the first page

Your screen should look like this after page numbering is turned off:

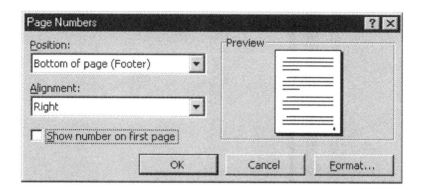

8 Click on **OK**

Your header will not print on the first page after following these steps.

🖱 Click on the **Print Preview** button in the Standard toolbar and look at the header as it will print in your document.

🖱 Click on **Close** to exit **Print Preview**

Your research paper does not require a footer so we will not create one.

Editing a Header

If you find that you have made an error in your header:

🖱 Choose **View** from the Menu bar

🖱 Click on **Header and Footer**

You will jump into the header area and can perform any edits that may be required.

If the header displayed on the screen is blank you are probably on the **First Page Header** which should be blank. Click on the **Show Next** button to get to the header you created on page two.

🖱 Make whatever edits are needed.

🖱 Resave your FULLTERM document after you have created the required header

🖱 Exit Word

NOTE TO THE STUDENT:

The steps for creating a footer are similar to creating a header. Here are the steps required:

1. Choose **View** from the Menu bar

2. Select **Header and Footer**

3. Click on the **Switch Between Header and Footer** button in the Header/Footer toolbar

4. Follow the same procedure you used to create the header

☞ **DO NOT create a footer in the FULLTERM document**

Things to Remember

Terms

Explain or define each of the following terms:

> Header
>
> Footer
>
> Suppress header or page number
>
> Flush right text

LESSON 28
INSERTING RESEARCH

In this lesson you will add the paragraph that you composed from your Internet research to FULLTERM, add the reference to the Works Cited page, and sort the Works Cited page to put the references in alphabetical order.

Inserting a New Paragraph

Read through the FULLTERM document and find the best place to insert your newly composed paragraph from your Internet research.

To insert the paragraph in the selected location:

- Move the cursor to the left margin in the document where you want the new paragraph located
- Press the **Tab** key to indent the paragraph
- Type the new paragraph
- Be sure to insert the reference in parenthetical notation at the end of the paragraph

Add a reference

- Move the cursor to the end of the Works Cited page
- Type the Reference in the proper format, as indicated in the research section; Press **Enter** to end the reference

Sorting a Page of References

- Move the cursor to the first reference listed on the Works Cited page, at the left margin. DO NOT include the Works Cited title.

🖑 Point and drag with the mouse to highlight all the references on the Works Cited page

🖑 Click on **Table** in the Menu bar

🖑 Select **Sort**

This is what the screen should look like:

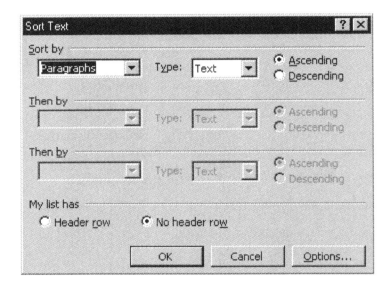

🖑 Be sure that **Ascending** is marked. We want the references to be in alphabetical order

🖑 Click on **OK**, the new reference will be moved to the proper alphabetical location

🖑 Click anywhere on the page to turn off the highlight

The Works Cited page references should now be in alphabetical order.

🖑 Resave the FULLTERM document

🖱 Close the document and Exit Word

Things to Remember

Terms

Explain or define each of the following terms:

      Insert

      Sort

      Ascending

      Reference format (Research lesson)

LESSON 29
EDITING A DOCUMENT

In this lesson you will edit the FULLTERM document that has been proofread and marked in a manner similar to that of a first draft document returned by an English Composition instructor. You will make the indicated changes and save the updated document copy. A copy of the proofread FULLTERM document can be found in Appendix A in the back of your book. It contains a list of Proofreader's Marks that are provided to help you understand the indicated changes. Use these marks as a guide to make the needed changes to your document. Remember, the copy of FULLTERM in Appendix A does not include the paragraph that you have composed and inserted into the document. The previous lessons have provided you with the skills needed to clean up your document.

You will change the left and right margins of the FULLTERM document. The Word default left and right margins are set at 1.25"; MLA format requires 1" left and right margins. The default font size in Word is 10; this font is too small for the MLA format. You will change the font size of the FULLTERM document to 12.

🖐 Open the FULLTERM document on your disk

Change the Left and Right Margins

Move the cursor to the top of the FULLTERM document.

🖐 Click on **File** in the Menu bar

🖐 Click on **Page Setup**

Your screen should look like this:

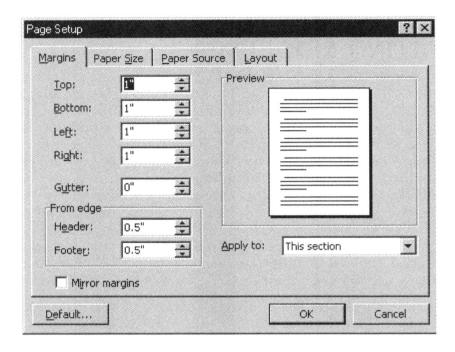

🖰 Click on **Left**, change it to 1". You can either type 1" in the window or click on the down indicator at the right of the window until 1" is shown in the window.

🖰 Click on **Right**, change it to 1". You can either type 1" in the window or click on the down indicator at the right of the window until 1" is shown in the window.

After you have made the changes to the left and right margins, your screen should now look like the example above of the Page Setup box.

🖰 Click on **OK**

Changing the Font size of the document

Make sure that your cursor is at the top of the FULLTERM document.

🖰 Click on **Edit** in the Menu bar

🖰 Choose **Select All**; the whole FULLTERM document will now be highlighted

🖰 Click on the **Font size** window arrow box in the Formatting toolbar

This is what the screen should look like:

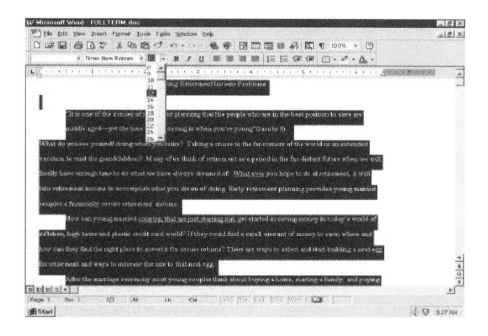

🖰 Point to **12** in the pulldown menu; Click

This is what the screen should look like after you have changed the font size:

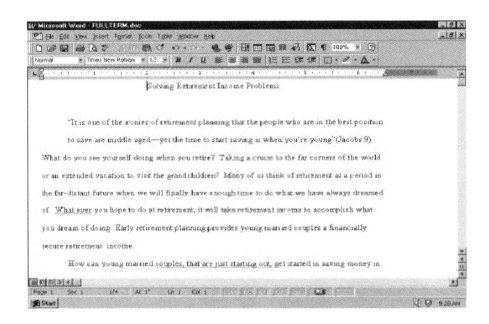

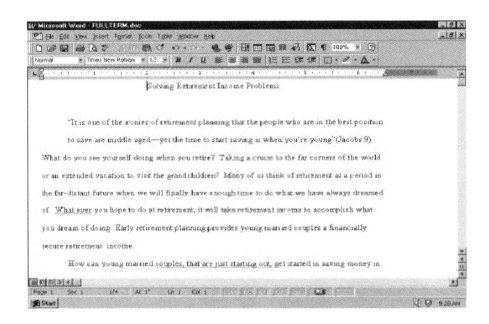 Before going any further **Save** the changes you've made in the FULLTERM document

Make the Proofing Changes to the Document

 Make the changes indicated in Appendix A

Remember, in the Works Cited page, all colons should be followed by **two** spaces.

Hanging Indent

The Works Cited page of the document should show the second line of every reference indented 5 spaces. This is called a hanging indent.

Let's create a hanging indent.

✍ Move the cursor to the left margin of the first reference line on the Works Cited page, on the B in Burchell

✍ Point to **Format** in the Menu bar; Click

✍ Choose **Paragraph**; Click

The window on your screen should look like this:

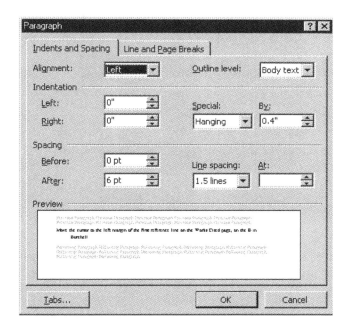

✍ Click on the **Special** box in the window

✍ Choose **Hanging** from the list; Click

✍ Click on **OK**

Your screen should look like this, showing the Burchell reference as a hanging indent:

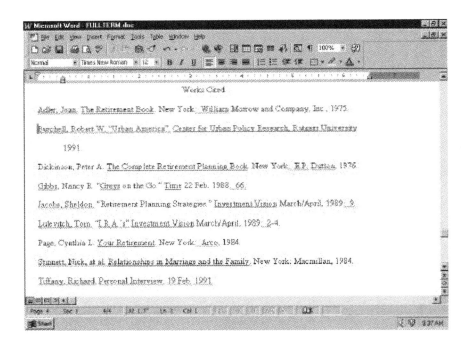

 Follow the preceding steps to create hanging indents for any remaining references that have two lines of text.

You will now run the Spelling and Grammar Checker again. The Grammar Checker does not like two spaces after a colon, but it is required; Ignore these suggested changes on spaces. Remember not all suggested changes are best for your document, you must decide which are needed.

If the Grammar Checker finds two words that should be combined into one, make these changes. An example of this situation was shown in the TERM1 document in Lesson 25.

Check with your instructor if you have questions concerning grammar rules or specific problems in your document.

✆ Start the **Spelling and Grammar Checker**, check for any errors that might be found in your document after the editing process.

Once you have completed the changes to your FULLTERM document, be sure to save it.

✆ Resave the FULLTERM document

✆ Close the document and Exit Word

Things to Remember
Explain or define the following terms:

Delete

Insert

Backspace

Cursor movement

Center

Underline

Hanging indent

Spacing following a colon :

LESSON 30
A COVER PAGE

In this lesson you are going to create a cover page for your research paper and put the required leading information on the first page of your document.

Requirements for the Cover Page

1. A cover page should have a five inch top margin, the contents should be double spaced, and each line should be centered.

2. The first line of the cover page contains the title of the paper.

3. The second line contains the student's name.

4. The third line contains the instructor's name.

5. The fourth line contains the course number.

6. The fifth line contains the course title.

7. The sixth, and final, line contains the date.

Creating the Cover Page

The cover page should be a separate document, **not** part of the FULLTERM document.

Be sure you are starting a new Word document.

The default font size is incorrect for the cover page. You want the font size to match the font size in your FULLTERM document, which was 12.

✐ Click on the **Font size** arrow box in the Formatting toolbar

✐ Highlight **12**; Click

The font in your new document should now be Times New Roman 12.

Change the top margin:

- Point to **File** in the Menu bar; Click
- Select **Page Setup**
- Change the **Top** in the Margins window from 1" to 5" by typing a **5**

You do not need to change any of the other margins.

- Click on **OK**

Change the line spacing

- Select **Paragraph** from Format in the Menu bar
- Follow the steps you've learned to change the Line Spacing from single to double.
- Click on the **Center** button in the Formatting toolbar

Every line that you type will be centered. End each line by pressing ENTER.

Now type the title of the paper as the first line of the document.

- Type: **Solving Retirement Income Problems**
- Press **ENTER** twice to create the quadruple space before the next line
- Type **Your Name** (please type your actual name, not the words Your Name)
- Press **ENTER** six times for the needed spacing before the third line
- Type the **instructor's name** (again, the actual name of your instructor)

🖑 Type the course number, **English 102**

🖑 Type the course title, **English Composition**

On the last line of the document you want the current date:

🖑 Select **Date and Time** from Insert in the Menu bar

This is what your screen should look like:

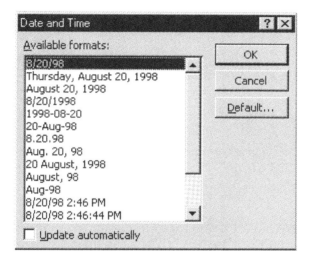

🖑 Choose the format that spells out the month, shows the day, then the year (example: November 4, 1998)

🖑 Click on **OK**

The cover page is now complete.

This graphic that follows shows what your cover page should approximately look like.

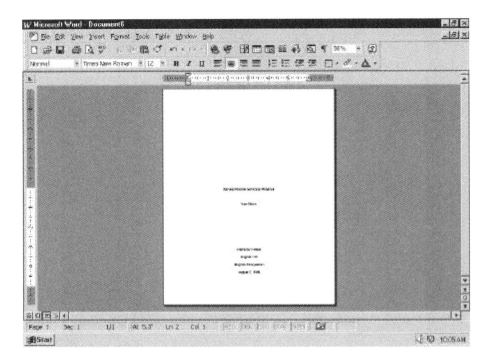

The above graphic is showing the cover page in Print Preview mode, so you will not be able to read it, but you should be able to get a sense of the overall layout and form.

🖱 **Save** this document on your disk with the name **Cover**

🖱 **Print** the Cover document

🖱 **Close** the Cover document

Required block of heading information

Now you need to create the required information heading for the FULLTERM document. This information IS NOT a header.

Be sure you are starting with a blank screen.

🖱 **Open** the FULLTERM document

- ⌐ Place the cursor at the top of the document

- ⌐ Press **ENTER**

- ⌐ Press the   up arrow to be back at the top of the document on the blank line

We don't want this information centered. We want it left aligned.

- ⌐ Point to the **Align Left** button in the Formatting toolbar; Click

The cursor should be at the left margin.

- ⌐ Using the skills you have acquired throughout previous lessons, create the heading information (**NOT A HEADER**) on the first page of the FULLTERM document.

The information should contain your name on the first line; the course number (English 102) on the second line; the instructor's name on the third line; the current date on the fourth line; and an extra blank line on the fifth line. Remember that the document is double spaced so there will be a blank line between each of these lines of text.

This is how your document should look containing this heading information:

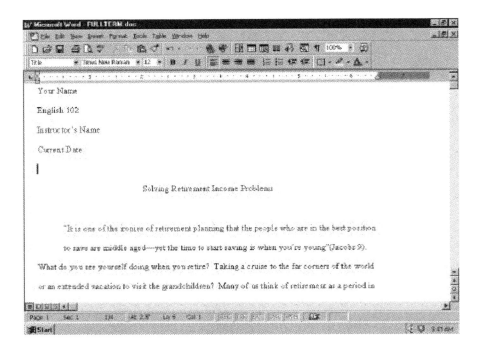

🖰 Resave the FULLTERM document on your disk.

🖰 Using **Print Preview** view your FULLTERM document to make sure that the heading is in the top left corner of the first page. Also ensure that the document is double spaced; and that the header that you created containing your last name and the page number appears on the second page and all following pages.

If your document does not meet these requirements, use the skills you have gained in previous lessons to fix whatever is needed.

🖰 **Print** the FULLTERM document

🖰 Close and **Exit** Word

Things to Remember

Terms

Top margin

Center

Line spacing

Close a document

Insert a blank line

APPENDIX A

⌃	Insert comma	⊥	Push down space
⌄	Insert apostrophe	⊏	Move to left
" ⌄	Insert quotation marks	⊐	Move to right
⊙	Insert period	⊔	Lower
⊙	Insert colon	⊓	Elevate
;/	Insert semicolon	sp	Spell out (U.S.)
?/	Insert question mark	stet	Let it stand
Delete		Caps	All Capitals
Close up		lc	Set in lower case
Delete and close up		#	Insert space
∧	Insert (caret)	Transpose (retrieve, only is)
¶	Paragraph		
no¶	No paragraph; fun in		

317

GLOSSARY

=AVG()	A Microsoft Excel 97 function to calculate the average of values in a range of cells.
=COUNT()	A Microsoft Excel 97 function to count the number of values in a range of cells.
=MAX()	A Microsoft Excel 97 function to calculate the largest value in a range of cells.
=MIN()	A Microsoft Excel 97 function to calculate the smallest value in a range of cells.
=SUM()	A Microsoft Excel 97 function to sum the values in a range of cells.
Absolute Value	Is a cell reference or address used in a formula that will not change when copied. For example the formula =$C$4-C5. The $C$4 cell address is absolute.
Analog	A computer which does not count in two digits but continuously measures and compares changing values.
Application	A practical use of a computer. Applications let us perform a variety of tasks from playing games to creating a letter or doing bookkeeping for a business.
Application software	Software that directs the computer to perform specific tasks. A word processing program is an example of application software.
Arithmetic-logic unit (ALU)	The computer's circuitry for arithmetic, comparative, and logical functions. The

	ALU is an integral part of the computer's microprocessor chip.
ASCII	The American Standard Code for Information Interchange, a standard code adopted to facilitate the exchange of information between computers and various types of computer programs.
Auxiliary storage	Any storage medium, such as disk or tape, that is long-term and nonvolatile and is not directly accessed by a computer's microprocessor.
Binary arithmetic system	The basis of operation for digital electronic computers. Binary arithmetic uses only two digits, 0 and 1 which represent on and off.
Bit	A binary digit; the basic unit of data recognized by a computer. Bit is short for binary digit.
Booting	The process of loading the operating system into a computer's memory.
Byte	A unit usually containing 8 bits. Each byte contains the information necessary for identifying a single character.
Cell Pointer	The dark thick border around the current cell.
Cell	Is the intersections of a column and a row. It is the area where we can enter data.
Central processing unit (CPU)	The central component of computer hardware, containing circuitry that controls the interpretation and execution of instructions. The CPU consists of the control unit, the arithmetic-logic unit, and main memory.

Chart Type	The format of the chart. There are many chart types to display worksheet data.
Chart	A graphic representations of data in the worksheets and/or workbooks.
Column	A vertical range of cells in a worksheet. A column is designated or named by alphabetical character(s).
Command line interface	An interface between the operating system and the user that requires a typed command to issue instructions to the computer; one of three types of human-computer interface.
Command	An instruction issued to perform a specific task or function. Commands are usually either typed at the keyboard or chosen from a menu with a keyboard or with an alternative input device such as a mouse.
Computer literacy	Being knowledgeable about the computer and how it works in our daily lives; also, being able to operate and use a computer, at least to do basic tasks.
Computer system	A system that consists of people working together with software and hardware components to process data into useful information.
Computer user	A person who works with a computer system to achieve a desired result.
Computer	A device that does three things: accepts structured input; processes it according to prescribed rules; and produces the results as output.
Context Sensitive Help	Activated with the F1 key, Context Sensitive Help takes the user to the

	place in the help menu located within an operation or command.
Control unit	One of three components of the CPU, it directs the step-by-step operation of the computer by directing electrical impulses among itself, the ALU, and main memory, and between the CPU and the input and output devices.
Copy	To duplicate data or a file. It usually involves placing the duplicate into memory and placing it to another location.
Current Cell	The cell with the cell pointer on it where Microsoft Excel 97 performs present action(s).
Cursor	Typically, a blinking rectangle or underline that indicates where the next keyboard character typed will appear on the screen.
Data entry	The process of entering data into computer memory.
Data processing	The process of using specific procedures that turns data into useful information for people.
Data	The raw material of information. Data include facts and numbers suitable for communication or interpretation.
Database management system	
(DBMS)	A computer system that lets the user organize, store, and retrieve information from one or more databases.
Database	A common pool of data--a single, common storage entity used by a DBMS.

Default File Location   The location that is used if the user makes no other choice. For example, if you wish to save a file and you do not change to another drive or directory location to save the file.

Delete   To erase or remove data or a file.

Digital   A computer that uses the binary arithmetic system to perform arithmetic and logical operations on data.

Disk drive   An auxiliary storage device that reads data from a magnetic disk and copies it into RAM, or that writes data from RAM onto a disk for storage.

Document   A file created by application software, consisting of text, numbers, sounds, video, or graphics.

DOS (disk operating system)   The major PC operating system; an integrated set of programs that perform three important tasks: providing access to the various operations of the CPU; controlling the peripheral devices; and, offering a variety of application program support services.

Dot-matrix   An adjective applied to video and print hardware that forms characters and graphic images as patterns of dots.

Downloading   Transferring files from a large, central computer to a small, remote computer.

Edit   To make any change of content in a document or file. The extent of an edit can range from the addition of a single comma to a massive reorganization and rewrite.

Electronic mail	The transmission of messages over a communications network. Electronic mail, or e-mail, is a computer-to-computer version of interoffice mail or the postal service.
Ergonomics	The study of how to create safety, comfort, and ease-of-use for people who use machines such as computers.
F2 Key	A function key which puts Microsoft Excel 97 into edit. It allows you to edit the data in the current active cell.
F5 Key	A function key which allows you to move the cell pointer to another cell on a worksheet or workbook.
Facsimile (fax)	Transmission of pictures, maps, letters, and so on via telephone lines from a sending fax machine to a receiving fax machine.
File	A complete, named collection of information, such as a program, a set of data used by a program, or a user-created document. A file is the basic unit of storage that enables a computer to distinguish one set of information from another.
Filename	A unique name used to identify a file. In Windows 95, a filename must have at least one character but not more that 255 characters, followed by a period (or dot) and three-character filename extension.
Floppy disk	A flexible plastic disk, coated with a magnetic substance and usually encased in a protective plastic cover.

Folder (directory)	A catalog for filenames and other directories stored on a disk; way of organizing and grouping files on a disk so that the user is not overwhelmed by a long list of files.
Font	The style and format of letters used in documents. Letters with the same font can be of different size, or may be bold, italic, or underlined.
Fonts	A family or collection of printed characters of a particular size and style.
Format	The pattern in which data are stored on a disk; a command used to organize and design text as it appears on the screen or as it is printed. Changing the format of a document does not change the content of the text, only the way the text looks.
Formatting	When applied to a document or worksheet it refers to how the document looks. For disks, it refers to preparing the disk for use.
Formula	A rule expressed as an equation, useful for calculating. A mathematical statement that describes the actions to be performed on numeric values.
Formulas	Used to perform math on values in cells.
Function	The purpose of or the action carried out by a program or routine; a general term for a subroutine; in some languages, a subroutine that returns a single value. In a spreadsheet, a process or program that generates a mathematical result or value.

Functions	Built-in formulas and operations in Microsoft Excel 97 allow the user to do special operations without setting all the individual properties each time.
Graphic user interface (GUI	A type of display format that enables the user to choose commands, start programs, and see lists of files and other options by pointing to pictorial representations (icons) and lists of menu items on the screen.
Graphics	Pictorial representations of data produced by data processing; images such as line drawings and photographs that are comprised of more than text characters.
Hanging indent	A type of indent that places the first line of a paragraph at the left margin, and subsequent lines at a specific tab stop.
Hard carriage return	A return entered at the end of a paragraph by pressing the ENTER key.
Hard copy	Printouts of computer data in readable form, such as reports or listings.
Hard disk drive	An auxiliary storage device, usually found inside the system unit, that uses a metal disk coated with magnetic film for data storage. A hard disk can store much more data than a floppy disk.
Hard page break	A page break forced by entering a command. A hard page break is not moved when text is added or deleted above it, or repaginates the document.
Hardware	The physical equipment that makes up a computer system--the machine itself, including chips, circuit boards, key-

<table>
<tr><td></td><td>board, disk drive, monitor, and other components.</td></tr>
<tr><td>Help</td><td>Allows the user to find help using the HELP from the menu bar or by clicking on the icon and clicking on the needed icon or tool bar item. Context Sensitive Help is activated with the F1 key. Context sensitive help takes you to the place in the help menu where you are within an operation or command.</td></tr>
<tr><td>Home</td><td>The home location in any worksheet is cell A1.</td></tr>
<tr><td>Home key</td><td>A key between alphabetical keys and the 10 key pad used to move the cell pointer to cell A1</td></tr>
<tr><td>Human-computer interface</td><td>The way the computer and its software are presented to the human being who is about to use them.</td></tr>
<tr><td>Icon</td><td>A picture or a graphical representation to convey and idea or a concept. Icons can be a button, found on a toolbar, or used in a graphical user interface to represent a task or command</td></tr>
<tr><td>Impact printer</td><td>A printer whose printing device comes into contact with the paper to form a character, such as a dot-matrix printer.</td></tr>
<tr><td>Information</td><td>Data made meaningful through interpretation by people.</td></tr>
<tr><td>Input device</td><td>A hardware component used to enter data into a computer. The keyboard is a common input device.</td></tr>
<tr><td>Instruction</td><td>A group of characters, bytes, or bits that defines an operation to be performed by</td></tr>
</table>

a computer. Instructions are often in the form of programs, telling the computer what to do with data.

Integrated circuit (IC)
A complex electronic component that performs key functions in computers and other devices; also called a chip.

Integrated software
A group of individual software applications capable of freely exchanging data with each other; typically a combination of word processing, spreadsheet, DBMS, and graphics.

Justification
Is used to align text or values in a document or cell. The icons indicate left, center, right, or full justification. They are found in the formatting tool bar.

Keyboard
A hardware component used to enter data and instructions into computer memory; an input device.

Label
Used a text in a document or a worksheet. Microsoft Excel 97 can not complete a mathematical function to a label.

Laptop
A small personal computer, often powered by batteries or rechargeable cells, that is portable and can be used in remote locations.

Laser printer
An output device that prints by directing a laser beam onto a rotating drum, creating an electrical charge that forms a pattern of letters or images.

Legend
Used to help describe or identify elements or items in charts and graphs.

Local area network (LAN)	A type of private network, interconnected by dedicated communication channels, that allows a group of users in a small geographic area (such as a room or building) to share data, programs, and hardware resources.
Logical operations	Computer operations that test and make decisions by comparing values.
Main memory	Also called primary storage or random access memory (RAM); the main general-purpose storage region to which the microprocessor has direct access. A computer's other storage options, such as disks and tape, are called secondary storage.
Mainframe	A large high-level computer designed for the most intensive computational tasks. Multiple users connected to the computer via terminals often share mainframe computers.
Mathematical operations	Adding, subtracting, multiplying, and dividing.
Media	The material on which computer instructions and data are recorded, such as floppy disks, magnetic media, and paper.
Memory	A computer system's storage facilities. Memory stores instructions and data in the computer.
Menu-driven interface	A human-computer interface that presents a list of the commands, tasks, or projects the user most frequently works with, developed to make the command line interface easier to use.

Microcomputer	A personal computer designed for use by a single individual, usually small enough to fit on a desktop.
Microprocessor	An integrated circuit used to perform arithmetic, logic, and control functions in a microcomputer CPU, or used as a control unit in a variety of electronic devices.
Minicomputer	A medium-sized computer, introduced as an alternative to the mainframe and used for a variety of tasks. Also called a mini.
Mode Indicator	Located in the lower left corner; indicates the action of the current menu choice, or process.
Modem	Modulator/Demodulator. A device which connects a computer to another computer through a telephone line.
Monitor	A hardware component consisting of a video display screen, where the computer displays input and output.
Motherboard	The computer's main circuit board containing the primary components of a computer system, such as the CPU, memory chips, and expansion slots.
Mouse Pointer	Indicates where the mouse is on the screen. In Microsoft Excel 97 it can be a large block arrow, large block cross, or a bold plus sign, with arrow heads horizontally. These different pointer types differentiate between what action will occur when using a mouse.
Mouse	A small pointing device used to effect cursor movement, so named because it

slides over the desktop and has a wire, or "tail," attached to the computer.

Multimedia	An interactive form of application that lets people and the computer engage in an ongoing exchange or presentation of information.
Networking	Linking computers through telecommunications hardware, software, and media to share resources and data.
Nonimpact printer	A printing device that forms characters without striking the paper, such as laser and inkjet printers.
Nonvolatile memory	Memory that stores and retains programs and data even after the computer is turned off.
Operating system	Part of a computer's system software that controls the execution of computer programs. The software responsible for controlling the allocation and usage of hardware resources such as memory, central processing unit (CPU), disk space, and peripheral devices.
Output device	A peripheral device that produces the results of data processing in a form humans can perceive. Common output devices include monitors and printers.
Overstrike (typeover)	A method to make changes in a document or worksheet. You can switch from insert to typeover by using the insert key. The insert key is a key between alphabetical keys and the 10-key pad.
Peripheral devices	Input, output, and storage devices such as disk drives, printers, modems, and joysticks, that are connected to a com-

puter and are controlled by its micro-processor.

Personal computer (PC)   A computer designed for use by a single individual and usually small enough to fit on a desktop; also called a microcomputer because it is smaller than a mini-computer.

Print Preview   The icon allows the user to see what the document or worksheet will look like when it is printed. It is a good idea to use this feature because it will save paper. You may also use Print Preview by using File on the menu bar and then Print Preview from the corre-sponding pulldown menu.

Printer   A hardware component that provides a copy of a computer's output on paper.

Program   A set of instructions that tells the com-puter what to do and when to do it. Programs are subdivided into systems programs, like the operating system, and applications programs used for word processing, spreadsheets, DBMS, or graphics.

Programming   The process of translating a problem or task into a language the computer understands.

Prompt   A character or message that tells the user the computer system is ready to accept a command or input.

Random access memory

(RAM)   Read-write memory, the "working mem-ory" of the computer, into which appli-cation programs are loaded and execut-

	ed and hold data currently in use. RAM is volatile memory and also called main or primary memory.
Read-only memory (ROM)	Memory permanently programmed with one group of instructions that can be read by the computer, but not written to. It is not lost when the computer is turned off (nonvolatile) and cannot be changed by the user.
Relative Value	A cell reference or address used in a formula that will change when copied. For example the formula =$C$4-C5. The C5 cell address is a relative cell reference.
Retrieve	To transfer a file from a disk into the computer's memory.
Revising	A word processing feature that allows you to check, change, and modify the text you have written; also called editing.
Root folder (directory)	The primary, highest-level (top most) directory, it often contains one or more subdirectories.
Row	The horizontal division of cells on a spreadsheet program. Together with columns, rows form the spreadsheet matrix. Rows are usually numbered down the left side of the screen with row one at the top.
Save As	This allows the user to give a name to a file that has never been saved, or to re-name or relocate a file when it is re-saved. Use File on the menu bar and then "Save As" from the corresponding pull down menu.

Save	The icon saves the current file back to the default, the place where it was loaded from or saved to before. You may also save a file using File on the menu bar and then Save from the corresponding pull down menu.
Saving	Storing the contents of main memory on a disk or other nonvolatile, auxiliary storage device.
Scroll Arrows	Buttons located at the ends of the scroll bars that control the movement on the document or worksheet window. Click on the arrow to move the window up or down.
Scroll Bar	The bar at the right or bottom of the screen that controls the movement to the document or worksheet window, using the Scroll Arrows or Scroll Box.
Scroll Box	The box in the scroll bar that controls the movement on the document or worksheet window. Grab the box and drag the box to move the window up or down.
Scrolling	The process of moving data vertically on the screen to permit viewing of any desired portion.
Sector	A pie-shaped wedge that compartmentalizes data into addresses for the disk drive head to locate.
Silicon ship	A thin piece of silicon on which electronic components are etched. An inte-

	grated circuit that uses silicon as its semiconductor material.
Software	Computer programs; instructions that cause the hardware--the machines--to do work. Usually divided into two categories; system software and application software.
Spreadsheet	An application that uses mathematical formulas to perform a variety of accounting and mathematical calculations. Also, calculations on data arranged in a matrix or grid; the software version of the paper ledger sheet.
Stand-alone program	An application that is used by itself and does not share data with any other application.
Storage device	A peripheral device used to store computer data, such as a floppy disk, hard disk, or magnetic tape.

Supercomputer   The largest, fastest, and most powerful type of mainframe computer often used in government and science research facilities.

System software	Programs that run the computer system or aid programmers in performing their work. The operating system in system software.
System unit	The main system cabinet in a personal computer, typically housing the power supply, the motherboard, and one or more storage devices.
Tip Wizard	An optional tool bar that gives tips and helps to the user.

Track	A path along which data is recorded on a continuous medium such as a magnetic tape or disk.
Uploading	Transferring files from a small, remote computer to a larger, central computer.
Utility software	Software that provides commonly needed services, such as copying data from one storage device to another. A program designed to perform maintenance work on the system or on system components--for example, a storage backup program, a disk and file recovery program, or a resource editor.
Value	A number. In spreadsheet applications values take two forms. One is the constant, the raw numbers or data entered for processing. The other is the mathematical formula used for performing calculations on the constants.
Virus	An insidious program that enters computer systems via other programs or through communications networks, hides itself, infects the computer, and causes damage.
Volatile memory	Memory that stores and retains programs and data only when the computer's power is turned on.
Wide area network (WAN)	A type of private network that uses phone lines, microwave relaying stations, and satellites to connect computers over a wide geographic area.
Window	A portion of the video screen dedicated to a specific purpose.

Word processing	A software application that lets users write, revise, format, and print text for letters, reports, manuscripts, and other written documents.
Word wrap	The word processing program's ability to calculate whether the word being entered will fit onto the end of the line. If not, the word is automatically moved to the next line.
Workbook	A Microsoft Excel 97 file that contains worksheets and charts.
Working Directory	The default directory where data, files and temporary files are stored
Worksheet	One sheet of a workbook where data is entered, calculated, or graphically displayed.
WYSIWYG	The acronym for "what you see (on the screen) is what you get (on the printout).